Praise for *The Agile Culture*

"This is the Agile book I've been waiting for. Enough with the rituals of process. Let's get into what really matters—creating the culture that teams need to thrive."

—Marty Cagan, founding partner, The Silicon Valley Product Group

"A book full of practical tools and real-life stories—a great resource for every leader involved in a serious Agile transformation."

—Hendrik Esser, director of portfolio and technology management, Ericsson

"'What is culture? How do we create a culture? What are our cultural problems?' These questions can have lofty, philosophical, theoretical answers that sound profound. Unfortunately, profundity rarely gets the job done. The authors have once again broken an important topic into easily understood parts. Not only do they make the questions understandable, they provide specific, actionable techniques for answering the questions and addressing the challenges. This book is as much a how-to as it is a what-is-it and a why-do-I-care book. Everybody who is in a leadership role, or deals with people in leadership roles (that'd be just about everyone, right?) should read this."

—Steven "Doc" List, vice president of learning, Santeon Group

"The content is phenomenal! Just an incredible distillation of years of experience."

—Christine DelPrete, senior director of technology, Amirsys, Inc.

D1567687

THE AGILE CULTURE

THE AGILE CULTURE

LEADING THROUGH TRUST
AND OWNERSHIP

Pollyanna Pixton
Paul Gibson
Niel Nickolaisen

✦✦Addison-Wesley

Upper Saddle River, NJ • Boston • Indianapolis • San Francisco
New York • Toronto • Montreal • London • Munich • Paris • Madrid
Capetown • Sydney • Tokyo • Singapore • Mexico City

For information about buying this title in bulk quantities, or for special sales opportunities (which may include electronic versions; custom cover designs; and content particular to your business, training goals, marketing focus, or branding interests), please contact our corporate sales department at corpsales@pearsoned.com or (800) 382-3419.

For government sales inquiries, please contact governmentsales@pearsoned.com.

For questions about sales outside the U.S., please contact international@pearsoned.com.

Visit us on the Web: informit.com/aw

Cataloging-in-Publication Data is on file with the Library of Congress.

ISBN-13: 978-0-321-94014-8
ISBN-10: 0-321-94014-8

Text printed in the United States on recycled paper at RR Donnelley in Crawfordsville, Indiana.
First printing, February 2014

To my mother, an amazing woman. And to the McKinney family, who have taken me in as one of their own.
—Pollyanna Pixton

I dedicate this book to my wife, Carrie, who has been my companion, my help, and my support for the last forty years and without whom none of this would have been possible.
—Paul Gibson

This is dedicated to my family and friends—the people who have helped me have a wonderful life.
—Niel Nickolaisen

Contents

FOREWORD

"It's all about the people . . . ."

Change, or any transformation activity, is daunting. As experts tell us, "You don't change people, you can only change the process." So how do we, as leaders, motivate and inspire our employees and organizations to change?

Command and control leadership limits creativity, broad thinking, and the ability for us, as leaders, to get the most out of the talent in the organization. The Millennials that we hire today are very social, and they interact and learn through social means in a very virtual and boundaryless hierarchy. Large organizations, by their very own weight, are not nimble. But in today's social/cloud/mobile world, organizations need to experiment and pivot more rapidly. To compound this dilemma, process tends to govern too tightly, with every exception or edge case being overmanaged. Process becomes a controlling means to an end and not a guideline. Organizational outcomes tend to be measured in vanity metrics. Trust is completely eroded, and creativity is muffled.

Dealing with this requires a shift in our leadership model: a move from command and control to a collaborative model that builds trust and pushes ownership and decision making deeper into the organization, while retaining a good balance of process and policy. The outcomes demonstrate an organization with energy and creativity, surfacing the talent and resilience to innovate and pivot as the business dictates.

I like this book, and the authors, because these ideas have been applied successfully with groups within IBM and within elements of Pitney Bowes. With the help of many employees who piloted the initial workshops, the authors polished many of the early models and refined them to the point where they were able to publish them for this book. Additionally, the authors provide metrics that can help you know whether you are on the right path to building a high-performing, collaborative team and creating a culture of trust.

Now, what do I have to say about the authors and why I admire them for writing this book? Paul Gibson and I worked together from 2007 to 2010 at IBM. He is truly a proper British gentleman. He helped me with the Agile adoption initiative—during which we trained, in 18 months, more than 8,000 employees on Agile approaches—resulting in over 60 percent of projects using Agile. The success of the Agile adoption is directly correlated to his passion and commitment to the IBMers and their wanting to get off the dreaded six-month project death marches. As we rolled out Agile at IBM, it highlighted the need for better communication and collaboration. This is how I met Pollyanna Pixton and Niel Nickolaisen.

The mold was broken when Pollyanna Pixton was born. For a person of short stature, she packs a mean bark but no bite, and a sense of having fun all the time. Her passion is improving leaders and giving them tools to succeed. I met her at an Agile conference and sat through her "Collaborative Leadership" lecture, in which she spoke about moving away from command and control to collaborative leadership. I thought this would dovetail nicely with the work Paul and I were doing at IBM. Pollyanna had cofounded Accelinnova with Niel, so they came as a package deal. Niel, another proper gentleman, but from Utah, created a model to help teams set priorities and backlogs, and that ensured that teams were building value, not just building stuff. When an opportunity presents itself, I fondly goad Pollyanna as she and Niel teach collaborative leadership. I tell the participants that Niel's content is "hard but straightforward" and Pollyanna's is the soft, fluffy stuff. If you want to see a short woman, dressed in black, go ballistic, just tell her that she teaches only "soft" stuff.

These three folks are dear friends who have helped me through my own transformation, and I thank them for that. The models illustrated in this book show how leaders can overcome obstacles (people or process) they face to build a culture of trust and high-performing collaborative teams.

I hope you enjoy the book and have the opportunity to apply the concepts. I certainly make every effort to apply them at each company I'm at or to each client I'm working with.

—*Sue McKinney, vice president, engineering backup and recovery at Symantec, and former Pitney Bowes and IBM vice president of development*

PREFACE

Given today's rapidly changing business cycles, it is essential that leaders transform their organizations to be value-driven, responsive, and incredibly agile. The largest barrier to Agile adoption is not knowing how to change the culture to one focused on learning how to delight customers. This book provides and explains tools and models that leaders can use to create the vision for and implement this culture transformation.

It is not easy to go from a date-driven, internally focused culture with its false certainties to a value-driven, customer-focused, agile culture. Given the choice, most people choose the status quo. Many people go kicking and screaming through the transformation. Some people or organizations won't make the transition at all. Through our experiences in technology companies (IBM, Pitney Bowes, and others) adopting Agile, we have developed a set of proven tools to help organizational members at any level create a culture that embraces and fosters Agile methodologies and delivers products customers love. These tools lead to a culture of continuous innovation, transparency, trust, living with uncertainty, proactive risk management, and improved decision making.

Value Proposition

This book is a handbook on how to create, move to, and maintain a culture of energy and innovation. We cover

- Creating a culture of trust.
- Helping teams take ownership and not taking it away from them.
- Aligning the goals of the teams with the business goals of the organization.
- Dealing honestly with ambiguity and uncertainty.

We start by setting the stage in Chapter 1, Unleashing Talent, by discussing why we need to unleash the talent of everyone in the organization and why the combination of a culture of trust and everyone knowing and owning results is the foundation for innovation and motivation.

Then we turn to an in-depth discussion of the Trust-Ownership Model in Chapter 2, Trust and Ownership. In Chapter 3, Building Trust and Ownership, we look at how to create, maintain, and move to a culture of high trust/high ownership. This includes the need for business alignment and for dealing honestly with ambiguity and uncertainty. The tools you will need for trust and ownership are found in Chapter 4, Trust Tools, and Chapter 5, Ownership Tools. In Chapter 6, Business Alignment Tools, we cover tools to help you ensure your goals and the goals of the team are aligned with the goals of the business. Chapter 7, Dealing Honestly with Ambiguity, presents the tools to deal honestly with ambiguity and uncertainty.

It is not an easy transition. Many people don't want to change. Many believe that if things are working effectively enough as they are, why should they do something differently? When this happens, we call it "hitting the wall"—a term we use to describe any obstacles and resistance you find to changing the culture. Where the walls might appear and what to do about them are covered in Chapter 8, Tools to Deal with Walls.

Metrics are important in assessing and driving progress, but metrics can be a wall if they work for the old culture but do not work for the new state. We dedicate Chapter 9, Metrics, to developing metrics for the optimal culture and discuss why they are important.

Finally, we provide an extensive case study in Chapter 10, Case Study, that covers all the principles in this book, helping you to see how you can use them in your organization.

Because many of the tools have multiple uses in getting you to Energy and Innovation, Appendix A, Quick Reference Guide, is a quick reference highlighting which point (trust, ownership, alignment, or ambiguity) the tool applies to and in which chapter its use and description can be found. Appendixes B through E provide worksheets, processes, and metrics for helping you move in the right direction.

ACKNOWLEDGMENTS

Group Acknowledgments

As a group, we would like to thank Todd Little for pushing the edges of our model, asking hard questions, and helping us sort through the ins and outs of our ideas. He was a great help in scaling our ideas and giving focus to the book. His review comments were invaluable.

Marty Cagan has been a champion of agile cultures for many years. We were delighted when he reviewed our book and passed on valuable insights to make this work even better.

John Lynch, Hendrik Esser, and Steven "Doc" List reviewed from an "agilista" leadership point of view, as their work is in the development of leaders who support agile teams and methodologies. Their contributions helped us clarify many sections and concepts for our readers. We also had excellent reviewers and editors from Pearson who spent hours helping us get our ideas correctly on paper.

We have a much better book because of the help from them all. Thank you.

Pollyanna Pixton

About my coauthors: The world is so lucky to have Paul Gibson in it. His view of the world and his wise words have expanded the way I see things without criticism. "It's not complicated" are words from him that always bring ideas to light. Niel has been in my corner for many years, always asking "How can I help?" What great friends, with such integrity and honesty, always pushing me to learn more and try to be humble.

I have the support of many amazing friends: Sue McKinney, who provided the opportunity to us to try out these tools in the organizations she has led. Greg Carlisle, over distance and time, has always been there with kind words, encouragement, and love. Imogene and Michael Rigdon have seen me through so much of my life's journey with understanding, compassion, and fun. Sally Bosken saved my sanity in high school and has been there ever since with the right words and a good laugh when needed.

Todd Little provided insights into our models in this book as he tried to "break" them, looking to ensure we have it covered. He has been a pal of constant conversation and exchange of ideas for years. When I stumble, he is there to catch me and assists me with seeking self-forgiveness.

Leo and Jean Gallagher are the true definition of the word "neighbors." They are always there when I need something, offering support, kindness, stromboli, and the "occasional" bottle of wine.

I have spent many long hours working alone with only my delightful dog, Missy, to keep me company. Throughout all my ranting and raving, she never complained. What a perfect companion.

Paul Gibson

First, thanks to all my colleagues and friends I have worked with throughout my career. You have individually and jointly taught me so much.

Thanks to the leaders I have worked with, who inspired, trusted, and challenged me with great opportunities. Your guidance and examples are the foundation of this book. Especial thanks to Geoff Robinson, Kristof Kloeckner, Bill Woodworth, Pat Sueltz, and Sue McKinney, who all showed me just how good leadership can be.

Thanks to Ted Rivera, my coconspirator in our round-the-world Agile training sessions. I learned so much from Ted, and it was a special time of my life that I will never forget.

Thanks to Mary and Tom Poppendieck, who introduced me to Lean Software Development and who were so generous with their help and support.

Finally, I owe so much to my coauthors, Pollyanna and Niel. They opened my eyes to the power of collaboration and culture. Their experience, knowledge, and insight have been profound, their discussions always rewarding, and their friendship delightful. Without them, this book would never have been written.

Niel Nickolaisen

I would like to acknowledge my close and fun working relationship with both Pollyanna Pixton and Paul Gibson. I met Pollyanna about ten years ago, and knowing her has led to many interesting learning experiences. Paul Gibson is one of the great people on the face of the earth. The world would be a much better place if everyone were like Pollyanna and Paul. I would also like to thank my staff and the president of my organization, who gave me the time to contribute to this book—and I promise the writing never got in the way of my work! I have had the pleasure of working with and learning from a variety of great leaders—without them, I would be nothing.

CHAPTER 1

UNLEASHING TALENT

The Big Ideas

- In today's rapidly changing world, we need to unleash the talent of everyone in the organization.
- The combination of a culture of trust and everyone knowing and owning results is the foundation for innovation and motivation.

Who Moved My World?

Perhaps it has always been this way: Some organizations rise and then fall; others do well, plateau, and then somehow hang around; still others bring it together and then stay for a long time as leaders. However, today these cycles move *so* much faster. We often joke that the title of the next great business book should be "Good to Great to Gone."

In our quiet moments we ponder the reasons for this acceleration in hopes of finding ways leaders can help their company succeed.

Certainly the ubiquity of technology drives part of the change. Every aspect of life is now digital: the books and newspapers that some of us still read; the games we play; the way we communicate with each other and our customers—it has been years since we *wrote* a letter. The work tools are now all digital. We review and approve expense reports from the tiny screens of smartphones—usually while pretending to listen to coworkers during a meeting! A common theme among technology analysts is that the technology part of the marketing budget will soon outgrow the budget of the IT department.

Consider also the ways in which we are incredibly connected. We can collaborate with almost anybody in almost any way at any time. We now pull off major projects with people we never meet in person. The ease and fluidity of collaboration mean that ideas flow much faster and get implemented much faster. All of this has us hurtling onward.

We also think the instant availability of any and all services contributes to the constant dynamic nature of this new normal. There is no need to wait for the things that used to take some time—and thought. If you need a new business application, one exists for you from someone. If you need to create a new application, the development, test, and production environments are just a website and a credit card away.

The net result is constant change at an increasing pace in an environment of incredible uncertainty.

Just a few years ago, a major consumer technology company was declared to be the most innovative company on the face of the earth. Today, the same people who made that claim are saying that the company has lost its way. What happened? A competitor developed a new product that is taking market share away. We suspect this cycle will continue and include other companies that come up with something new and amazing.

With technology everywhere and changing all the time, our jobs, customers, and competitors can change in an instant. In this world of rapid change and ambiguity, what hope do we have of keeping up? What can we possibly do?

We propose that in the midst of this accelerating change, some things become very important.

The Power of Trust and Ownership

Now more than ever, we need to unleash the talent of individuals, teams, and organizations. This might be the only hope we have to not just survive but thrive. But, too often, we put a wet blanket over the fire of innovation and motivation. In the midst of uncertainty, we attempt to control outcomes by controlling actions. In a state of fear, we insist on obedience to what has worked in the past—even if it no longer works. We somehow believe that rigidity results in predictability. Worried about the future, we become opaque rather than transparent with our teams. And when push comes to shove, we doggedly trust just ourselves and our instincts.

We have always believed that no one person can know everything and needs to rely on the talents of others to be successful in a role, on a project, or in the marketplace. With the increasing pace of change, trusting each other is critical. It is impossible for a person to know it all and do it all when it is all different.

We maintain that highly motivated individuals and teams who are passionate about delivering results will figure out what to do and make sure the right things get done. If such people understand what needs to be done and why it needs to be done and have the tools to succeed, miracles seem to happen. And, given the ambiguity that accompanies the decisions we make, we need such miracles.

We wrote this book for two reasons. First, we want to share with you the power of leading with Trust and Ownership. Second, we would like to provide you with specific, pragmatic tools we have used—and believe you can also use—to create a culture of Trust and Ownership. The combination of Trust and Ownership unleashes individuals, teams, and organizations to do amazing things—even and particularly in the face of rapid change and uncertainty.

Let's start with an example of how one rather unremarkable e-commerce team used Trust and Ownership to do something that had never been done before.

The company was deeply worried about customer retention. In parallel, the e-commerce product team had low credibility. After all, thought company management, customer retention is low because the web team is just not that good. When we say that the e-commerce team was unremarkable, we mean that the team was stocked with good, solid, hard-working, capable people. Not a single member of the team would have initially been considered some king of e-commerce or a customer retention superstar. The team had been through its share of turmoil. The company had tried different leaders and structures. They had moved the team into and out of different parts of the company. But not much changed. Some members of the team found other jobs and quit but most stuck around. Like we said, rather unremarkable. Finally, because nothing else had worked, the company became desperate and moved the team to be part of the information technology (IT) department. After all, e-commerce used technology; therefore, IT seemed the natural place for the team. This was not a conscious move but it started the team and the company on the path to doing what had never been done before.

The head of the IT department, the chief information officer (CIO), was not sure what to do with the team and so put the entire lot into the application development team. Steve, the newly announced manager of the application development team, took the change in stride and, not knowing any better, treated the e-commerce team like everyone else in his group. Let's pause for just a moment. He treated them like everyone else in his group. What did that mean? Steve was a leader who believed in the power of Trust and Ownership. He did not pretend he knew much about e-commerce (although he did). He did not believe the word on the street that the e-commerce team was ineffective or rudderless. He treated them the same way he treated everyone else. Steve figured that all the team needed to thrive was to own the results (but what results?) and to be trusted.

Steve met with each member of the team individually and then met with them as a group. In every encounter with them, he affirmed that he knew they were talented and knew what to do. He spent time with them explaining the company's goals and how both the IT department and the application development team directly supported those goals. He encouraged them to think big—really big. He asked them to link their work to the company goals. He shared his concerns about customer retention. He did not offer solutions but asked questions like "When it is too late to recover a lost customer?", "When do you think a customer first starts to think about leaving us?", "What are the indicators that a customer is trending away from us?", and "How soon could we pick up those indicators?"

Steve posed such questions at what seemed to be random times. During a project review, Steve might gaze out the window and ask, "I wonder if there is a way to detect customer dissatisfaction before customers even make their dissatisfaction known to us?" He would then return to whatever he had been doing. But the team got the message; Steve was somewhat consumed with customer retention.

Steve showed the team he trusted them. This did not mean he was soft or a pushover. If the team told Steve that they would get something done by Friday, Steve expected it would be done by Friday. If it was not done by Friday, he wanted to know why. Steve did not accept excuses. If the team did not deliver, Steve wanted to know what the team would do differently the next time to make sure that they would keep their commitments. But if the team told Steve what they would get done, he left them alone to do their work.

Steve pushed ownership to the team. If the team had a problem, Steve would help them diagnose the issues without telling them what to do. He would say things like "This one is going to be a real challenge. I am really interested in what you come up with the solve it." At first, the team was not comfortable with this approach—after all, the team had been kicked around enough that their confidence was low. But as time went on and they resolved issues, their confidence grew. As confidence grew, the team started to think about customer retention. After all, they were the e-commerce team. Customers used their products to search, review, reject, and purchase the company's products. If they did not have insight into the mind of the customer, who did?

As the team worked on various projects, they thought about how those projects might be used to somehow, someway improve customer retention. The only data available to the team were traditional web analytics and click stream data. This helped them understand the navigation and friction points with customers. Could they leverage this to improve customer retention? In their product and project planning, they started to brainstorm about customer retention. They started by asking some "what must be true" questions. In their case, what must be true in order to detect which customers are thinking of leaving us? They jotted down things like

- We need to know their previous buying patterns.
- We need to know their previous website navigation patterns.
- We need to know their full customer service history.
- We need to know what products they returned.
- We need to be able to match the patterns of similar customers.
- We need to profile customers into behavior patterns.

In reviewing their list, they realized there was a whole bunch of information that they needed but did not have—yet.

Their next what must be true question was "What must be true in order to get this information?"

This list included

- We need to rope people into the project who can get us the information.
- If we don't have the information, we might need to develop ways to get the information.

Their final what must be true question was "Even if we have the information, what must be true in order to use it?"

They had only one answer to this question: We need analytical tools that we can use to profile and then predict the behavior of individual customers.

At this point it was time to talk with Steve. The team met with Steve and walked him through their approach and logic. Steve offered a suggestion here or there and then asked, "What do you need me to do in order to move this forward?" The team needed someone on the project who could get the team the information. They would also need Steve to allocate budget for any analytical tools. Steve told the team that a member of the data team had expressed interest in doing some type of customer analytics and told them to see if they could convince this person to join. As you might expect, this person came immediately on board.

Having assembled the team, the group now needed to figure out how to operationalize their approach. They were dealing with an incredible amount of uncertainty. First, would the approach even work? Second, could they get the data they lacked? Third, would the data be meaningful enough to provide insight? Fourth, would the analytical tools work? Fifth, would the analytics yield answers that would increase customer retention? How could they best deal with this massive uncertainty? It was time to spend more time with Steve.

The team presented these challenges and asked for advice. "Hmmm," answered Steve, "when I am confronted with a lot of uncertainty, I think of how I can break things into phases. During each phase, I eliminate at least one element of uncertainty. So you might want to think of what small steps you can take now—no need to invest a great deal of resource until you have more confidence that this will work—to find out what will and will not work. You can then increase your investment as uncertainty declines."

The team got back to work and laid out what they thought was a logical, phased project plan that moved the project toward the end goal while also reducing the uncertainty of the future phases. They returned to Steve and showed him the plan. Steve asked some questions that helped the team refine the phases and they started work.

In the first phase, the team assembled the data they thought they needed. Most of the data was available but not in a consumable form. So the team took a slight detour and added a phase that incorporated data conditioning to the project. The first phase also identified a significant gap in the data. In order to group customers into similar patterns and profiles, the team wanted to get demographic and psychographic data that the company simply did not have. How could they get this? How much of this data did they need? And could they get by without it?

They identified their options:

- They could, at a pretty high cost, buy the data. But it might be foolish to incur the costs on an analysis that might not even work.
- They could buy the data for a subset of customers and use this as a test to validate the approach.

They had agreed to purchase the subset of the data when a member of the team asked, "How many of our employees are also customers? If there are enough of us, could we collect the data from employees and use that as our data subset?"

The data team ran a query that showed enough employees were also customers. But how would they get the employees to offer up their personal data?

The team went back to Steve and explained what they wanted. Steve thought, "Interesting idea but how do we get the employees to participate? We are pretty early in a very uncertain project. If we tell employees what we are doing, are we setting an expectation we might not meet? Or is this a way to get everyone invested in thinking about customer retention?" Steve offered to run the idea up the management chain. In selling the project, Steve kept things at a very high level and repeated, over and over, the experimental nature of what they were attempting. He assured everyone that their personal information would be secure (and it would).

Enough employees participated that the project moved forward. The team now had the data but needed to do the analysis. The company had some analytical tools but not anything that would do the type of profiling and predicting the project needed. What to do now? Someone suggested another meeting with Steve. Someone else said, "No, we can figure this one out ourselves." Several team members volunteered to do the research to see what was available—at a very low cost—to do such analyses.

When the team got back together, they had identified a couple of open source options they could use to test their approach.

The results were encouraging. Several clear patterns emerged. Other patterns were mixed or confused. But the clear patterns were compelling enough to ramp up the investment and try data with non-employee customers. The company agreed to start by purchasing the external data for a subset of customers. The company also agreed to acquire advanced, non-open-source technology—on a trial basis—to do improved analytics on customer retention. Over the next several months, the pilots and tests continued and expanded with improving results. Throughout all of this, Steve remained tightly connected to the project team, not to tell them what to do but to guide and focus them on the desired outcome—improved customer retention. Steve also removed any barriers and championed not just the project but the project team.

This happened more than two years ago. The company and team have continued to refine the approach and the results. The company's customer analytics are so good that the company can tell during the first customer interaction with their website, with high confidence, which profile matches the customer. This profile defines the customer's buying motivation and purchasing triggers. The company appeals to this specific motivation in everything they do with that customer. The profile also tells the company the customer behaviors that indicate if the customer is trending away from the company. If the customer is trending away, the company invokes an intervention strategy specific to that customer type. Across all customer profiles, customer retention has increased an average of 12 percent, which has added millions of dollars to the bottom line. Along the way, the rather unremarkable e-commerce team—composed of the same people who were foisted on Steve more than two years ago—are considered geniuses in the company. Others seek them out for their opinions on a wide range of topics.

How did such a team and company transformation happen? Through the power of trust and ownership. Steve trusted the team to perform and built a very strong sense of ownership for company, departmental, and team results. This unleashed the team to become more than they had ever been. The team was motivated and innovative. The wet blanket of micromanagement was lifted off the team and life for everyone got better.

Please keep in mind that trust alone is not enough, nor is ownership. What matters is the combination of a culture of trust and a passion for delivering the right results.

Getting Started with Trust and Ownership

In today's incredibly fast-paced and competitive markets, how do we deliver products and services that delight? By unleashing the talent of every person in the organization and focusing them on shared ideas that generate meaningful business value and by trusting them. This creates a place where they want to be, not have to be. As leaders we can then step aside and let them do their work.

This sounds nice and possibly easy but many organizations fall short. We have seen them fail many times—too many times. The key to success is to create a culture open to the possibilities of change and innovation, one that can respond quickly to customer needs and wants, one that is agile.

What does this type of culture look like?

- Continuous definition of what is of value to customers and what will delight them, involving the customers and the entire organization.
- Delivering the right stuff when it is ready, when customers want to take it.
- Learning, learning, learning. Mistakes are accepted, not punished.
- Innovation is the accepted norm, not the exception.
- Everyone has what they need to succeed.
- Shared vision with all goals aligned with the business goals of the organization.

This works when the team has ownership of the solution (the "how" not the "what") and when leaders trust the team and support processes that demonstrate that trust. That's where we begin.

One look at the Trust-Ownership Model (Figure 1.1) makes it is clear where everyone wants to be: Energy and Innovation. But are you there? If so, you may not need to read further.

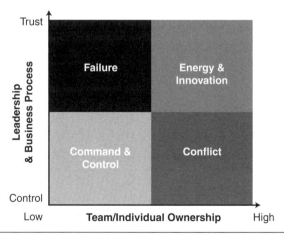

FIGURE 1.1   Trust-Ownership Model

But most of our teams and organizations sit in the Command and Control state, because living in Failure or Conflict cannot last for long. If the team is in Conflict, they will eventually get tired of the fight and start doing what they are told, moving to Command and Control. In Failure, leaders are afraid the teams will not deliver, so they increase control, again moving to the Command and Control quadrant.

Energy and Innovation is severely hampered in the high-control environment/culture. Such a culture can limit productivity and revenues [1, 2].

Because we find most cultures in Command and Control, if we traverse the diagonal in Figure 1.2 from high control/low ownership to the high trust/high ownership state, we create a culture that maximizes delivery and innovation. The further along the diagonal your organization can move, the more successful the business is in delighting customers, delivering value early and often, and increasing revenue.

Integrity is the foundation. Where is the integrity in telling the team they "must have all this done by this date" when you haven't asked the team if it is even possible? Or saying, "I want it done this way" without discussion and without considering there may be another, perhaps better, way? Setting unrealistic goals is dishonest and lacks integrity. Teams are very aware when this happens, and it leads to distrust and demotivation. Without integrity, you cannot create a high trust/high ownership culture.

However, the goals and purpose of all teams must align with the business goals of the organization. And to be a healthy organization, you must

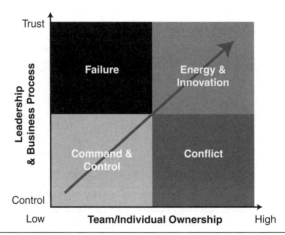

FIGURE 1.2 Moving to the green

deal honestly with ambiguity and uncertainty. With these things in place we have a high-performing organization, working together to provide value and delight customers.

Book Conventions

Before we move on to the next chapter, we'd like to describe our use of *we* and *I* in the stories and examples we use. The three of us (Pollyanna, Paul, and Niel) have worked together so much that we sometimes finish each other's sentences. We also sometimes work independently from each other. Writing this book created a bit of a challenge in how we relate our stories and experiences because sometimes we had the experience together and, at other times, the story belongs to only one of us. In an attempt to minimize the confusion but also be accurate in telling the stories, we developed what we hope is a simple rule of thumb. If two or all three of us were involved, we use *we*; if only one of us had the experience, we use *I*.

References

[1] Lyman, Amy. "The Trust Bounce." Great Place to Work® Institute, 2009.

[2] Chambers, Harry E. *My Way or the Highway: The Micromanagement Survival Guide.* San Francisco: Berrett-Koehler, 2004.

CHAPTER 2

TRUST AND OWNERSHIP

The Big Ideas

- To maximize productivity, a leader needs to build ownership within the team and act as an enabler rather than a controller.
- To enable the team, the leader must trust the team and create a culture of trust.
- Individuals and teams perform best when they understand "why" they are doing what they are doing.
- Working honestly with ambiguity builds trust and ownership, improving team productivity.

Some Teams Do Better Than Others

I always thought I was a trusting, collegiate style of leader until Human Resources organized a survey of those who worked for me.[1] Their view of my natural style was slightly to the right of Attila the Hun!

I have been working on improving the effectiveness of our development teams for many years—trying to find ways to deliver more value to our customers. I quickly recognized that iterative approaches with motivated and empowered teams were far more effective than the command and control method that I had used, and, I might add, with good success for many years. When I thought about it, it seemed strange to me that I hadn't realized this myself. I struggled to understand why it was not obvious that I should have built full ownership within the teams that worked for me.

---

1. As a reminder, if a story or experience involved all three authors, we use *we* in telling the story. If only one of us was involved—in this case, Paul—we use *I*.

I started by wondering what I had feared, why I hadn't given the teams more control over what they were doing. The answer came quite quickly. I was simply afraid that if I trusted them they might not deliver! I was scared! The command and control processes had worked well for me. Why should I give them up? Indeed, it was because of them that I had been promoted and had been offered many good opportunities.

I thought about the good managers I had worked for and who had trusted and supported me. Of course, I assumed, this was because they "knew" that I had ownership and therefore they could trust me. What had they seen that I had not?

I recalled Geoff, who gave me a senior management position in his lab. "Paul, there are only three things you need to do:

1. Build a great team.
2. Explain clearly what you need them to do.
3. Make them coffee. (Get them what they need to succeed.)"

Geoff practiced what he preached and was a joy to work for.

I took all of this input and went back to thinking about the relationship between my trust of the team and the degree of ownership of delivery that they had, and it crystallized in the Trust-Ownership Model I describe here. With that said, let's dive a bit more into this concept.

As we have worked on improving business effectiveness with small and large companies, we have run free-form brainstorming sessions with many teams and hundreds of managers from first line to executives. We ask *what behavior they would like **from their leaders** to help them be more effective*. The normalized results are shown in Table 2.1.

What do teams want from their leaders in order to be more effective? Trust—the clear winner by a factor of two, followed by Vision and Strategy. Even when the survey was done at different management levels, there was no difference in the responses. Everyone wants to be trusted by their leaders.

Additionally, we asked middle and senior managers another question: what they felt their teams needed from them. The winner was . . . Guidance! Interestingly, those who answered the questions immediately recognized the inconsistency of their positions. This disconnect between what we feel we need and what, as leaders, we feel our teams need is the core of the issue that faces us today. In an ever-increasingly dynamic and complex world, what is the role of the leader? What is the responsibility

Table 2.1 Normalized Results of Brainstorming Sessions

Area	Weight
Trust	100
Vision and Strategy	50
Clarity	32
Communication	28
Risk Taking	25
Support	24
Focus	22
Collaboration	21
Feedback	19
Decisiveness	18
Investment/Resources/Dollars	18
Empowerment	16
Leadership	16

of the team? How can we combine trust and ownership to improve agility and results—and in significant ways?

Above all, everyone (including leaders) believes that they can be more effective when trusted by their leaders, but leaders feel their teams need more guidance. How can we work this out?

The Trust-Ownership Model

If a member of the team asks the leader a question, does the leader simply tell the team member "what" to do and "how" to do it? Or is it better to trust the person to figure out "how"? What if the situation is an emergency and requires an immediate solution? Does the leader still offer guidance or is it better to quickly solve the problem? Also, what is the best way to develop talent on the team? By having the leader tell everyone how to do everything? Not likely. And, if the team is not improving, how can the organization hope to become a market leader?

To try to make sense of the interplay between trust and ownership and also to help both teams and leaders assess where they are and define a path to success, we have developed a Trust-Ownership Model to make the issues clear and to help leaders understand not only "what" they need to do to make their teams more effective, but also "why."

To streamline the text in the remainder of this chapter we will use the shorthand terms of Leader and Team.

By **Team** we mean the individuals and teams that actually do real work to create customer and business value. Sometimes this will be a single individual, but more often it will be a group of individuals who are doing this work together. It is not an organizational entity. It is an inclusive term that encompasses all individuals who actively create value even if they report to other parts of the organization.

By **Leader** we mean to include team leads, managers, senior professionals, and the business processes and tools they create to control their subordinates' activities. Leaders should be considered to be any person or process that has organizational power over Team. For example, an expense processing system is an instance of Leader because it implements the wishes of some executive in the organization.

In the Trust-Ownership Model we explore the interrelationship between the amount of trust that the Leader or organizational process has in the Team and the level of ownership and commitment that the Team has to the success of the project or business. Figure 2.1 provides a visual representation of the model.

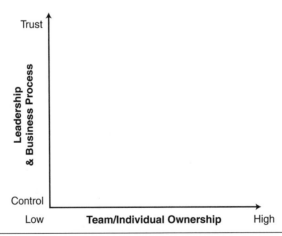

FIGURE 2.1 Trust-Ownership axes

On the vertical axis we note the amount of **trust** that the leader or business process has in the team or employee. Here trust is the opposite of control. Complete trust is equivalent to no control while complete control equals no trust.

Higher up the graph indicates that the behavior of the leader or business process demonstrates trust in those who are doing the work, allowing teams and individuals to take appropriate action as needed and own those actions.

As Leaders (including processes) move closer and closer toward control, we see much more management tracking, controlling, checking, and telling teams how to do their work. Teams spend more time documenting, reporting, and asking permission—wasting valuable time the team could spend on delivering business value.

Additionally, all decisions are made by the leader, manager, or system, causing a backlog and even more delay. The Leader has become the bottleneck, stalling work as the team waits for direction from the Leader.

Along the horizontal axis we look at the level of commitment and ownership of the team or individual who is doing the work. The left end is characterized by an attitude of "I'll only do what I'm told," while the right side represents the case where the individual is fully committed and does whatever is needed to meet the business goals that have been understood and agreed upon.

To simplify our discussion, we break the space into four quadrants (shown in Figure 2.2) and consider the activities and behaviors of the Leader and Team in each. We look at slightly extreme behaviors to make the salient points clear, but we do need to recognize that this is a simplification. In reality there are no actual boundaries. The degrees of trust and ownership, together with the behaviors, vary continuously along the axes.

We label the quadrants as

1. Failure (black)
2. Command and Control (yellow)
3. Conflict (red)
4. Energy and Innovation (green)

Now let's step through each quadrant.

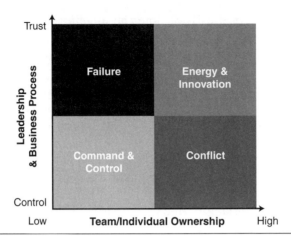

FIGURE 2.2   Trust-Ownership Model

Failure

In the upper-left quadrant, the Leader completely trusts the Team but the Team just doesn't care; the Team has no ownership or commitment to delivery. The Leader has abdicated responsibility to the Team but the Team feels no ownership of the outcome and is waiting for direction. No one is interested in delivering what the business needs, just delivering what they are told to deliver. Failure is inevitable.

I once worked with a team who didn't even know who their product manager was. They had funding for three people but absolutely no idea what their customers wanted. In the absence of any insight into the business goals, they were just doing what they felt like doing. The team was enjoying the freedom, but its members were frightened about their future. They were sure that once someone noticed them they would be in deep trouble.

For a committed Leader this quadrant is a very scary place. No Leader ever wants to fail. So, this *fear* of failure causes the Leader to take control. Note that this says nothing about the Team's *actual* sense of ownership. The Leader's fear, and possibly previous experience, requires him to take ownership because he *fears* the Team will not deliver. This, too, was my starting point at the beginning of the chapter.

Leaders act on the *fear* that Teams are not committed by moving to the Command and Control quadrant.

Command and Control

Unfortunately, this is a very common situation for Leaders. Driven by the fear of failure and a lack of trust in the Team, the Leader takes control.

Some years ago I was working with a senior vice president and was asked to prepare a series of communications for her. We discussed what was required, and I spent considerable time gathering the data and preparing the communications. We got together for what I thought would be a final review . . . and she tore it to shreds. She found fault with everything. She decided on a completely different form of report and rendered all the work I had done useless. A little later she did the same thing again and her team told me that this was just her normal way of working. The end result was predictable. I stopped doing good work for her. When anything was needed I just spent a few minutes putting something together in the full knowledge that she would change it all anyway. I don't know if she ever noticed.

Think about the leaders you have had in the past or have now. Did any of them tell you *"what"* to do and *"how"* to do it? Correcting you at every step of the way?

In the Command and Control quadrant the Leader's mindset can be described in the following way:[2]

- **The Team is less committed than I.** This is a particularly insidious but very pervasive belief in business and is often self-fulfilling. It is almost certainly untrue for the entire Team. It often is simply a reflection that it is the Team that has to face up to the realities of creating and validating a solution, while the Leader has little or no responsibility. If the Team identifies issues (not enough time, a lack of involvement by decision-makers, et cetera) that need to be addressed by the Leader, the Leader views this as lack of commitment. It may not be true, but perception often creates social reality.
- **I'm the Leader. I know what needs to be done and how.** This is a very dangerous assumption. While Leaders can be expected to have considerable self-confidence, they are often not aware of all the implementation implications. How did Leaders get into their leadership role? They got there by solving problems and delivering a great product. They have developed their skills of problem solving

2. A leader in this quadrant is defined by exhibiting any of the characteristics.

over years, and with their experience, often they do have great insight. However, even where Leaders have valid prior experience it is unlikely that their ability and knowledge outweigh the combined current knowledge of the Team. To compound this, recent research by Dachner Keltner at Berkeley and Deborah Gruenfeld at Stanford University suggests that as people gain power they tend to make decisions in less rigorous ways.

- **The Team cannot be trusted.** Many Leaders and organizations don't trust their people. Think of expense reports that require endless documentation to support every penny spent. What about purchase requests that require at least four levels of approval? This attitude is a hangover from the industrial era when it was assumed that employees were essentially lazy and would always follow their own selfish agendas. Strangely, in some leaders this belief applies not only to those below them in the organization but also to those above. Such leaders seem to believe that they are the only people capable of acting with integrity! In other cases, these leaders control out of fear—fear of those above them in the organization. For them, the drive for control is their only real chance to save themselves.

When Leaders think this way, it naturally leads to a set of behaviors built on their assumptions. In order to feel more comfortable that the business commitments will be met, the Leader often does the following:

- **Requires a detailed plan for everything.** This Leader wants to have everything worked out in advance so that he can critique it and be certain that all issues have been addressed. One team had to detail their efforts for every 15 minutes for two years! Seriously. In doing this, Leaders force plans to be inflexible and waste a lot of the Team's time doing detailed planning and estimating without honestly acknowledging that there is so much uncertainty that the plans are, at best, a guess. Remember, "It's a bad plan that admits of no modification" (from Publilius Syrus, 63 BC).

- **Tells the Team exactly "what" to do and "how" to do it.** This may be done via formal process; direct instruction; detailed plans, regulations, or objectives; detailed metrics; or implemented tooling. This vastly limits innovation and reduces—or possibly eliminates—the Team's ability to respond quickly to out-of-line situations. This behavior clearly tells the Team that the Leader has ownership of this project and that they do not. And, to make things even more controlling, the Leader tells the team "how" to do the work by defining every action, every step, and every method.

- **Asks for regular detailed status.** Because the Leader does not trust the Team he must know the status of every aspect of the work at all times. This way, the Leader can personally assess progress, identify issues, and direct action. Again the Team is given to understand that they are just agents of the Leader like pawns in a chess game. In many organizations this can lead to key Team members spending considerable amounts of their time creating reports and explaining progress details to the Leader rather than adding value to the project.

- **Inspects and checks every aspect of the activity.** As with status, the Leader is afraid of uncertainty and will put in place inspection and review processes that check up on the Team. The Team goal changes from meeting business or client needs to getting past the Leader's checklist. When a Leader has (possibly outdated) technical skill combined with directive behavior, the damage to the project can be considerable.

- **Makes all key decisions for the Team.** This slows down the delivery process considerably. The Team must ask for a decision: Should they do this or that? Where the situation is complex, they will often need to prepare multiple options for the Leader's decision. Waiting for a decision cuts deeply into the Team's progress.

- **Punishes failure visibly.** Built on the assumption that the Team cannot be trusted, the Leader feels it necessary to motivate Team members by punishing any that do not come up to the Leader's expectation or conformance to the defined plan. Many Leaders believe that this motivates the Team to deliver more.

All of these behaviors ensure that the Leader will have a full calendar: reading status reports, checking against expectations, checking each activity, and punishing the Team. And there is always a queue of people at the door asking for permission to take action. The Leader is a bottleneck, delaying the progress of the Team.

When Leaders act in this way it is not in isolation. Teams quickly learn what is expected and focus on making the Leader happy rather than providing value. The behavior of the Leader actually *generates* corresponding behaviors in the Team. The Team avoids decision-making. The Team also thinks less and innovates less. The Team complies. But, rather than turn off their brains, some members of the Team—probably those most important for long-term success—get frustrated and find ways to move somewhere else.

So the Team *learns* to

- **Believe that they don't need to understand the business.** If their Leader does not value this knowledge there is no need to spend any effort understanding business or customer needs.
- **Only do what it's told.** All the Team has to do is follow the Leader's direction. This is the way to be rewarded and avoid punishment. Do what the Leader requires and no more.
- **Believe that if something should fail, it must be the Leader's fault.** Naturally this must be true if the Leader makes all the decisions. The Team has done its job as long as it has done what the Leader directed. The result is not the Team's responsibility. It is easy to see just how corrosive this viewpoint is.
- **Not innovate or take risks.** In a command and control environment there is no place for individual innovation and risk taking. These behaviors only have a downside for the team unless permission is given in advance by the Leader.
- **Keep quiet about any issues.** Because the Leader checks everything, the Team's goal becomes to get past the Leader's checks. Nothing more. There is no benefit to the Team in exposing themselves to criticism or punishment by pointing out issues that might be attributed to them. The use of problems as opportunities for learning is completely lost.
- **Blame others for failures.** Finally, the Leader has created an environment where individuals play the blame game. If punishment is the norm then individuals are incented to identify faults in others rather than work together to overcome problems that occur in any project.

The Leader's untrusting behavior has actually *taken ownership away* from the Team. In this situation the Leader is teaching the Team that the Leader is responsible and not them. The Leader may in fact be more comfortable with this, but overall the Team is demotivated and project delivery slows. Most command and control environments operate at less than their optimum possible productivity. In order to avoid this situation, Leaders must rethink their role. Rather than being the ones who know everything and own every decision, the focus shifts to defining direction and creating the environment in which others will learn and make decisions. We dive deeper into this in subsequent sections of the book.

Figure 2.3 captures this Learning Spiral in a visual way.

1. The Leader's assumptions and underlying beliefs shape the way she acts.
2. The Leader's behavior teaches the Team what is valued and what is important.
3. The Team's understanding guides the way that they act.
4. The Team's action unsurprisingly reinforces the Leader's original assumptions.

Recognize that this Learning Spiral can work both positively and negatively. In the preceding examples, we showed how the Leader's negative views of the Team lead to a disempowered Team that just follows orders. In this situation everyone is dumbed down.

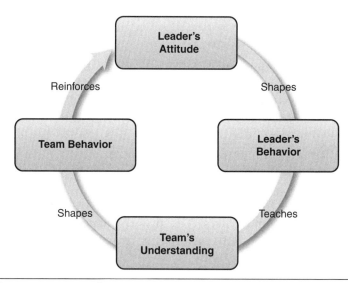

FIGURE 2.3   The Learning Spiral

Now consider the possibility of a positive spiral. The Leader's trusting approach and behavior teach the Team that self-reliance and ownership are valued, and these behaviors surface in the Team. This can work even for the fearful Leader as long as he acts in a trusting way, and the resulting Team behavior will help calm the fears and reward the Leader's trusting behavior.

Back to the negative spiral: We have all seen many instances where teams and individuals say, "I know this is madness, but it's what the leader or process or checklist requires."

Some years ago we worked with a large company that had produced a comprehensive checklist running to over 140 pages of criteria that projects had to fulfill in order to ship to the customer. A project manager was explaining to a director about a solution that had caused significant problems for customers and for the company in the marketplace after shipment.

"Were you aware of these problems?" his director asked.

"Yes, I knew the issues were there when we shipped it."

"You let it ship with errors?" The director was shocked. "Why didn't you fix the problems or at least warn the business?"

"It passed all the criteria, so we shipped it. If the issue is not on the checklist, it's not my problem, and it's not my job to decide what goes in the checklist."

The project manager felt that he had done his job well and wanted to be congratulated!

In the Command and Control quadrant, a Leader's untrusting attitude drives bad Team behavior, which reinforces the original untrusting attitude: a negative spiral that leads teams to the far lower-left corner of the Trust-Ownership Model and as far away from Energy and Innovation as possible.

"How many of you have ever worked for a micromanager?" is a question I often ask when I speak to a group. Usually, everyone in the room raises their hands.

"For those that have, how many of you enjoyed it?" All hands drop.

"What made it so bad?" The answers range from "I felt like my manager was telling to me to turn off my brain" to "If he wanted it done his way, why not just do it himself?"

A command and control environment kills both motivation and innovation. In this environment, persons are essentially told to turn off their brains, show up, shut up, and do what they are told. How motivated can someone be in such a situation? How much innovation will there be if only one person—the Leader—is allowed to think and create?

Most individuals and teams *do* care about what they are doing and *do* feel a strong sense of ownership. So what happens if the Team is actually pretty well motivated and really is committed to the delivery of the project but the Leader can't let go of Command and Control? We get conflict.

Conflict

This quadrant is characterized by continuous conflict between the Team and the Leader. Here the Team is committed, feels ownership, and *wants* to make progress but is continually held back by the Leader.

The Team is continually frustrated over spending scarce resources doing work that is not adding value to the customer: creating status reports, justifying positions, documenting options and recommendations for the Leader to choose between. Teams without trust also spend time discussing and documenting details with the Leader.

I was called in to help a project in this situation. The command and control leader had created a huge specification for an IT solution and wanted a full commitment to the complete delivery by a certain date, because he felt he had been let down by his IT team in the past. The team felt that there was considerable uncertainty in both the requirements and the solution and felt that it could not commit to the solution as defined. The result was a series of acrimonious meetings over many months and the project eventually ground to a halt and was abandoned. I helped the leader and the team to start again using an iterative process and coached the leader on how to build a culture of trust (See Chapter 3, Building Trust and Ownership).

Once iterations started, the leader was delighted to see the delivery of real value and began to understand the commitment of the team. To build confidence with the leader, the team relocated itself to the leader's business area. The end result was outstanding for everyone. The team delivered a solution very rapidly and went on to provide a series of enhancements that transformed their area of the business. The leader told me that the actual implementation of the first solution cost less than the write-off cost from the original contract negotiations.

Teams cannot stay in the Conflict quadrant. Either the Leader learns to let the Team have ownership and the Team moves towards the Energy and Innovation quadrant or the Team gives up and lets the Leader take ownership away from them, moving into the Command and Control quadrant.

Energy and Innovation

This is the place where *both* leaders and teams *want* to be. This is where things get done well and fast.

Here the Team understands the business and customer requirements and is working toward delivering the solution as rapidly as possible. Here the Leader has confidence in the Team and works at a more strategic level to help enable the Team to be more effective. The Leader is a resource for the Team for bigger issues and also has more time to think strategically about the marketplace and future opportunities. This is a wonderful place to be. As we have worked with individuals in many companies, everyone who has ever worked in or with such a team has told us that it was a delightful experience that they will never forget.

Who loves an audit? Once I was responsible for the internal audit program in our business, and it was a pain. We would plan a series of audits that visited each of the director's areas during the year. We were not welcome, seen as a painful distraction, and our findings were always disputed. Things had to change.

With the help of Colin, my lead auditor, we devised a completely new program. I announced to the board that there would be no more mandatory internal audits. We would arrange an audit only if a director invited us and asked each to name a person in their organization who would become their contact. Training would be arranged for that person and, in time, this would enable them to audit each other. Audit findings would no longer be reported to the board; they belonged to the directors for them to use as they saw fit. We would report only the training progress of their contact and the number of audits each director had requested.

The result was dramatic. Ownership was seen to be clearly with the directors and no longer with the internal audit function. We were welcomed in each area. We were seen as supporting and helping them meet their external audit readiness, and most important, the number of findings in external audits by prospective customers and the corporate team fell significantly.

In this quadrant, the negative spiral of behavior we saw in Command and Control is replaced by something much more positive. Here, the Leader's view can be characterized as the following:

- **The Team is committed to deliver what is needed.** They are a fully vested part of the business. They understand our strategy and direction. They know we work in a competitive marketplace and know who our competition is. They care.
- **The Team knows the actions that need to be taken.** The Team is skilled and knowledgeable. Collectively, they have the ability to deliver what is needed. If problems arise they can find effective solutions.
- **The Team can understand the importance of this project.** We have jointly discussed and agreed to the business, market situation, and customer goals. The Team understands and will engage and do the best work possible with the resources that they have.
- **The Team can be trusted.** They act with integrity and honesty. They meet their commitments.

From these beliefs the Leader builds a new set of behaviors that reflect a positive attitude toward the Team. The Leader knows that she needs to build the Team's capabilities and motivation. So the Leader

- **Helps the Team take ownership and doesn't take it back.** The Leader must not only state, but her actions must continually reinforce, ownership within the Team. The Leader is a valuable resource for the Team.
- **Conveys the vision, the value, and the urgency.** To reinforce ownership in the Team, the Leader has to give the Team as much understanding as possible of the overall project goals and context. This has to include the vision for the project and the competitive and business environment. If the Team is to be able to take appropriate and rapid decisions in line with the Leader's understanding of business and customer needs, the Team needs as much background information as possible.
- **Helps the Team focus.** Prioritization is always a challenge for any project. It is critical that everyone come to a common view of the most important features and capabilities to be delivered within the

limited timescale and resources. The Leader needs to be an active part of that discussion with the Team without taking ownership away from the Team. The best place for the Leader to do this is as part of the planning activities and in all the demonstrations of the deliveries.

- **Connects the customer with the Team directly.** One powerful way in which the Leader can help the Team take ownership is to find ways of building an ongoing dialogue between the Team and key prospective customers and users. This allows the Team to continuously refine the delivery at every level to ensure that it provides maximum value when shipped.

- **Enables the Team.** The Leader has to take a more strategic view of improving the capabilities of the Team. She needs to ensure that the Team is staffed and skilled, that it has the tools and resources to be effective, and that the overall organization supports rather than hinders the Team's delivery action. The Leader must become a resource for the Team.

- **Has time for strategic thinking.** The preceding activities will typically take significantly less of the Leader's time and effort than full-time project management. This frees the Leader to focus on longer-term business and market issues.

When a Leader acts in this way, the Team will respond by moving toward attitudes and behaviors that reflect the Leader's approach, taking ownership of delivering a solution that delights customers.

The Team does the following:

- **Takes ownership.** The Leader's approach encourages and enables the Team to do the right thing. They have been shown the customer and business needs and have the authority to act quickly and decisively.

- **Is accountable.** The Team understands that the responsibility and accountability are theirs. There is no safety net. They have signed up to deliver what they have committed to get done.

- **Can optimize what it does.** The Team can act quickly within the business constraints when issues are identified. The Team has the authority to modify its approach based on learning through the development cycle.

■ **Stands or falls together.** By being given ownership, enormous peer pressure for boundaryless behavior is engendered in the Team. By creating an environment like a small entrepreneurial company, the Leader helps the Team form into a cohesive, self-managing group.

The Trust-Ownership Model shows us that most Leaders and Teams reside in either Command and Control or Energy and Innovation. The Failure and Conflict quadrants are not stable, and Leaders and Teams cannot stay in them for any length of time. In Failure, where no one cares and no one delivers, the business will eventually cancel the project. Teams in Conflict eventually give up and hand control back to the Leader, losing productivity.

So what is the alternative? In Chapter 3, Building Trust and Ownership, we cover how to move from Failure, Conflict, and/or Command and Control into the green—Energy and Innovation.

Why Purpose Matters

We talk about, we think about, we debate about, and we hope for high-performing teams. Teams made up of individuals who are focused, motivated, and innovative. But focused on what? Motivated to achieve what? Innovative in getting to what? Owning what?

As we consider the Trust-Ownership Model, we optimize performance when teams and individuals "own" delivering results. But what results? Results aligned to purpose. We strongly believe—almost to the point of dogma—that a condition of becoming a high-performing team is to understand purpose. Purpose is the "why" and "what" of our work. When we understand purpose and align to it, we match the tens, scores, hundreds, and thousands of decisions we make to the goals of the project, the goals of the product, and the goals of the organization. If the purpose is nebulous or just plain wrong, it is either difficult to feel ownership for the results or we waste our ownership on activities that won't make a meaningful difference. For us, the word *purpose* indicates the real needs of the business— cutting through the opinions and territorialism and focusing on what will generate meaningful business value.

One of the critical tasks for a leader seeking to move organizations, teams, and individuals into the Trust-Ownership green zone of Energy and

Innovation is to clearly communicate, explain, and make clear the business purpose and goals. The goal of this critical activity is to articulate the purpose so teams can own delivery of the results—so they can filter and manage their activities to deliver work that directly supports purpose. This leadership role is very different from the historical role of leaders—which was often to lock purpose away and direct people to perform various tasks that they thought would deliver the business goals. In the agile, networked, innovative organization, the leader ensures that purpose is well understood so the teams can make decisions that lead to high-performance and desired results.

My team faced an enormous project backlog—new development, legacy enhancements, implementing agile methods, shifting resources into different roles such as business analyst and quality assurance, new software selection, and system implementations. It was difficult for them to fully understand this massive list of projects. Which ones were more important than others? Which ones required creativity? Which ones could be purchased rather than built, and so on? Without this understanding, they struggled with feeling ownership for the projects and their results. Working the portfolio would keep them busy, but would it keep them engaged and result in meaningful accomplishment? In my leadership role, I knew the best, fastest way to shift into a mode of accomplishment was to help the team understand the "why" of each project. To do this, I first had to get some clarity on the "why" myself. I met with my management team peers, and we defined three high-level organizational objectives. For our online, nonprofit university, these were the objectives:

- Improve graduation rates—this is our primary measurement of the success of our students.
- Improve operational excellence—we want to make sure that we become more efficient and provide improved service levels as we grow.
- Become an employer of choice—we want the university to have an innovative, high-trust culture.

I then met with the various project teams and explained why these objectives mattered to the future of the organization. If we improved graduation rates, our continued growth and success would be ensured. If we improved operational excellence, we would grow efficiently and not end up with complex, wasteful processes and practices that frustrated us and reduced our organizational agility. If we were the employer of choice, we would always be able to attract and retain the right people, and they would enjoy their work more each day. With this understanding in place, we mapped each and every project in the portfolio to one of these objectives.

Why were we redoing our entire analytics? Because the rebuild would give us information we could use to improve graduation rates. Why was there a project to implement a document management system? To improve operational excellence by automating a manual process that was becoming a bottleneck. We understood the "why" of everything on our backlog—all that work that we still needed to get done.

One of our projects was to outsource the management of our network. This was a very divisive project. The network administration team felt that this was the first step toward eliminating their jobs. As a result, they felt no ownership for the project and were doing what they could to slow down and discourage moving the project forward. But there was a very good "why" for this project (at least from my perspective). The team could not support many of the other projects in the portfolio because they spent the majority of their day in tier 1 and tier 2 support of the network—doing basic things like moves, adds, and changes. This type of work would be fine in the absence of all of the other projects that required their skills. What I had failed to do was explain why this project was important and how it would help us achieve one of the three objectives. So, I recovered my senses and met with the network team. I started by explaining the three objectives and how they mattered to the present and the future of the organization.

"How might this outsourcing project support any of the three objectives?" I then asked.

The silence was resounding.

I rephrased my question and tried again. "What are some ways we can achieve these objectives?"

Again nothing.

Because I had the time, I waited it out. Finally, one of the junior administrators ventured a connection.

"If we spend less time on the basic monitoring and management, we can work on the network upgrades we know will solve some of the nagging problems. I suppose that will improve operational excellence."

I wrote that one on the whiteboard and waited a bit more.

"Sometimes, we are too busy to respond to some of the basic and repetitive jobs like adding a person to the network—while they wait for us, they cannot do their work. Having someone else around to do those things would mean they get done faster—which improves operational excellence and also makes this a better place to work."

With these and a few other ideas, the energy rose and the group was soon discussing how best to manage the outsource relationship. The team completely took over the ownership of the project and kindly asked me to butt out. They now claim it was their idea and has been one of the most successful projects they ever initiated.

Later in the book, we introduce and describe tools we use to identify purpose—the "why" and "what" that help teams develop ownership. We use these tools to both define and infer how the organization creates competitive advantage. Thus, any person or team, at any level in the organization, can align to what generates business value. When this is clear, we start moving into the green of the Trust-Ownership Model.

The Trust-Ownership Model helps us recognize where we are and things we can do to change our results by designing a different operating system. The tools we describe in the other chapters of this book are things we can all use to accelerate the transition.

You Cannot Defy Gravity

It is time to face reality. And that reality is that the world has changed dramatically in the past decades and is continually changing at a rapid rate. First, computer technology came along. Then Al Gore invented the Internet and the world started getting connected. All that connection created globalization. Globalization meant that anyone anywhere could affect our businesses and business rules. Combined with ever-increasing technology innovation, the world is now much more dynamic, much more competitive, and a whole bunch less certain.

Yet, we strive for certainty. Many of our traditional management processes—from financial analysis to project management—are designed to create certainty. But in this age of rapid change and the resulting ambiguity, do these management practices work? Or do they merely create the illusion of certainty?

We were recently asked by the chief information officer (CIO) of a large, global company to help him and his staff figure out how to use iterative methods in the face of a capital budgeting process that required a five-year, predictable planning horizon. The CIO explained,

"We have to create a five-year cash flow projection for each of our major projects. We have no idea how to do that now that we are using iterative methods. We have been trying different things but can't get anything that is acceptable."

"Acceptable to whom?" we asked.

"To the CFO and the capital budgeting process. Before a project gets approved, we have to define the five-year costs and benefits for the project. But using iterative methods, we don't know what the final product will look like until we get past the approval stage. Prior to approval we can define an initial set of features and functions, but those might change during the project. If those change, the cash flows might also change."

One of the CIO's directors spoke up, "We are stuck. We cannot get approval without accurate cash flows, but we don't know the actual cash flows until after the project is approved and we have done a fairly large number of iterations."

What an interesting dilemma. The CFO requires a five-year cash flow so that the company can determine the net present value (NPV) of the IT projects. But using iterative methods, the final state of the IT project might be a bit (or more than a bit) different from what was initially planned, thus invalidating at least a portion of the five-year cash flow projection. Ideally, using such methods improves the NPV of the project as the project team adjusts to customer feedback and focuses on the features that generate the most value. But that is not the issue. The issue is that the CFO and company want to know, with certainty, what will be delivered and what the impact will be over the next five years. The CIO and his staff wanted to figure out how to deliver certainty while still using iterative methods.

We offered a different perspective and approach.

"When was the last time you gave a five-year cash flow projection that turned out to be accurate?" we asked.

The members of the team thought for a few moments and looked at each other. Finally, one brave person said, "We don't know—we've never looked at it."

"Has anyone ever looked at it? Does the CFO or his staff ever do a post-project analysis to see whether or not you got your five-year cash flow projections right?"

"I don't think so—at least no one has ever asked us for the data they would need to make the assessment."

"In that case, does it really matter what the impact is of using iterative methods on the CFO's process? I am not trying to be critical or flippant, but does it really matter what numbers you use in your five-year cash flow projection at all? It seems to us that because no one ever looks at it, make the number whatever you want. Or why do it at all?"

This conversation was making the CIO very uncomfortable. He and his staff spent a lot of time refining estimates to generate "good" numbers for the capital budgeting process. This process was one of the company's critical management methods. But was it doing any good? Did it make any difference in what the company did or did not do? Even worse, if there never was any real follow-through, how easy was it to game this process by inventing somewhat inflated cash flow projections in order to boost a project's NPV?

Sensing the challenges we had just presented to the CIO and his staff, we attempted to work toward a solution.

We are not saying that your estimates and this process are invalid. However, a useful process needs to recognize that the future is uncertain. I suspect it is nearly impossible to define what will be happening in the marketplace in one year—let alone in five years. Think back on how technology has changed in just the past year. Then in the past five years. When you proposed a project five years ago did you understand how data analytics would change? Or mobile? Or social? When you proposed a project one year ago, how much certainty did you have about not only technology but the competition? How has the company's focus changed in the past year? What ideas and processes did new employees or leaders bring with them? No, we are not saying that planning is not useful. Planning is very useful. Planning lets us sort through the range of things that might happen and prepare ourselves for what might change. Rather, we are saying that the planning process needs to recognize the impossibility of certainty. So instead of planning that anticipates no changes, accept ambiguity and incorporate it into your planning. In fact, if you recognize the harsh reality that almost nothing is certain, you break through to a higher level of organizational agility and leadership.

This is a strong and potentially unsettling concept—that by embracing ambiguity, we can improve results. How is this possible? Let's walk through the logic.

Ambiguity Is a Reality

It really is impossible to know the future. Some years ago, for one of my son's elementary school science projects, we tracked the accuracy of the local weather forecast. Every morning, we opened the weather forecast and recorded what the forecast said about the high and low temperatures and sky conditions for that day and then three and five days in the future. We then recorded the actual temperatures and sky conditions on those days. We considered the forecast accurate if the predicted temperatures were within three degrees of the actuals and if the sky conditions were within one grade of the actual sky conditions. (For example, if the forecast predicted sunny and the actual skies were partly cloudy, the forecast was accurate. But, if the actual skies were cloudy, the forecast was wrong.)

We conducted our experiment for an entire month. Over that time period, the same-day forecast was, as you might expect, reasonably accurate. The same-day forecast was on target over 70 percent of the time. The three-day accuracy was not as good, clocking in at around 50 percent accurate. The five-day forecast was the least accurate—barely over 30 percent.

Now, as a society, we have invested lots of resources to improve and refine our ability to forecast the weather—we make multiple decisions in our lives and in society based on the weather. We have lots of intricate, advanced systems to track weather and project the future weather. In spite of this significant investment, the forecast for the *same day* was wrong nearly 30 percent of the time. Are you kidding me? Wrong nearly 30 percent of the time? To predict what is going to happen over the next 18 hours? And what about the three-day accuracy? We have weather satellites that can see what is looming three days away and yet we get it wrong almost 50 percent of the time? Admittedly, the weather is a difficult system to predict—there are many variables that come into play. But our business environment is also an incredibly difficult system to predict. Will a customer, today, make a decision to purchase or not to purchase? Will the critical resources on our most critical project decide to have a bad day? Will that technology we are depending on not work? Will a human somewhere along the critical decision path change his mind?

The harsh reality is that we are immersed in ambiguity and uncertainty. At a minimum, accept this. Even better, embrace this reality and operate accordingly. If we refuse to embrace ambiguity, we increase the likelihood that we will be wrong more often than we need to be.

Embrace Ambiguity and Incorporate It into All We Do

We can build an appreciation for ambiguity into our leadership, plans, and processes. One of the most powerful tools for embracing ambiguity is using iterative methods. Agile software development is an example of such iterative methods. So is Stage-Gate for product development. Using these methods, we embrace the notion that we don't know the future and will get to the future in a step-wise fashion, learning from customers and the market and correcting as we go. We make global plans that define a goal or an objective. But we follow a path that takes small steps toward that goal—small steps so that we can pause, get feedback, learn, evaluate, and reorient ourselves after each step. This reduces our chances of being wrong about the product, the technology, the market, and everything because we incorporate feedback and learn and adapt.

Learn as We Go

There is value in learning. If, in our plans, we assume we are correct and will go from point A to point B with no variations, we are also assuming that there is no chance to learn and act on what we learn until after we arrive at point B. But in an environment populated with innumerable variables and changes, we can learn critical lessons along the way and make corrections. By embracing ambiguity, we embrace learning. Over time, individuals and organizations that learn and adapt get things right more often and things wrong less often.

All of this sounds fine, but in a world that seeks certainty, what can a leader or team do? We have found that a very good starting point is to experiment. Experiment with more frequent planning—and see if it improves results. Experiment with iterative methods and see if they make a difference. Experiment with delaying commitments until you know enough and see if that leads to success.

Dealing Honestly with Ambiguity

When I was in high school, we used to do physics experiments such as measuring how a spring extended when weights were added. When I wrote up the final report, I was expected to make estimates of the amount of error in the measurement or I was likely to receive an F. That was in high school and yet executives and managers running small and large businesses continually ask for certainty in their decision-making process.

Does the following sound familiar?

"How long will it take to deliver this?"

"Hmm. I don't know for sure as I haven't looked at it in detail but I'd guess four to six weeks."

"Okay, I'll take the four weeks."

Or

"What revenue do you expect from this investment?"

"Well, we don't know for sure yet as we haven't yet had any statistically valid customer feedback, but I'd guess around $10 million plus or minus 20 percent."

"Okay, we'll accept your commitment of $12 million."

Or

Some time ago I was discussing with the CFO how his company made investment decisions. I asked whether the company asked for uncertainties or error estimations in inputs to the decision.

"Oh no. The engineers and business teams are always trying to add plus or minus figures to their numbers and dates, but I've told the staff to remove all of them. We need aggressive commitments."

What that CFO and other leaders need to realize is that this approach is *guaranteed* to make the team set *less* aggressive targets. If the business will not honestly accept uncertainty, then teams and individuals will always adjust their estimates to give themselves some buffer.

Building an organization where honest acceptance of uncertainty is the normal behavior is one of the essential foundations of both good leadership and getting teams and individuals to take ownership of the effective delivery of business value.

In an organization that practices honest acceptance of uncertainty you see the following behaviors:

- Individuals and teams share as much information as possible. Openness is the norm.
- Individuals and teams face up to the real situation and consequently can take the most effective action to deal with problems.
- There is no game playing or manipulation.
- Problems are discussed openly with a view to identifying the most effective solutions. There is no blame game.
- Uncertainty is both acknowledged and accepted.
- It is all right to identify and voice risks. It is also all right to take chances as long as they are visible and understood by all.

The Leader's Role

Effective leaders build this environment by example. They deal honestly with uncertainty and ambiguity in a way that is visible and obvious to their teams—and encourage their teams to do the same.

Effective leaders do the following:

- Acknowledge the difference between opinion and fact. Many discussions get heated because people tie themselves to opinions.
- Accept, and practice, changes of position and opinion as new information arrives. This demonstrates that they are part of a learning culture.
- Expect success, accept mistakes, and avoid blame.
- Recognize that a plan is just a current outlook. The project will make the maximum progress that it can, and it is highly unlikely to exactly match any plan. Don't force an aggressive plan. If one is needed, ask the teams to work out the best one they can. Join in the discussion and accept the risks.
- Do not ask for certainty and commitment where it is not possible. Otherwise, teams think they are being set up and will, at the very least, add large buffers to protect themselves.
- Consciously consider risks. Effective leaders recognize they cannot prevent all risks. They accept risk where appropriate. If an accepted risk comes about, they accept the cost of rework.
- Where firm dates or sizes are needed for interlocks between parts of the organization, they look for alternative mitigation rather than requiring dishonest uncertainty or spurious accuracy.

Please note that even when leaders embrace ambiguity it will take some time for the team culture to mirror the leader's behavior. Even a single instance of negative behavior can do real damage and encourage the team to fall back to game playing.

In summary, actively embracing and leveraging ambiguity and uncertainty provide valuable competitive advantage.

If the future is uncertain (and it almost certainly is), plan big but take small steps.

Take a hard and honest look at your processes to determine which ones ask for certainty when certainty is not possible—these processes are likely time and resource wasters.

To honestly deal with ambiguity requires a deep culture change—and this starts with leaders and the examples they set.

A Foundation of Integrity and Honesty

Let's pause for just a moment and talk about integrity and honesty. How do you define integrity? Pollyanna defines it as the opposite of manipulation. Paul defines it as an unflinching view of reality, and Niel defines it as holding to your standards—even under the most intense pressure. Everyone has a different take but basically it is honesty.

In the Trust-Ownership Model, integrity and honesty matter. Why? We cannot create or maintain a trusting environment if we do not operate with integrity and honesty! It is that simple. If the leader is not trustworthy, how can there be trust? If the organization lacks integrity, how sustainable is the team's ownership of the results?

Likewise, integrity and honesty mean that we are honest about reality. This includes not only reality about our current results and what we must do in order to change those results but also the reality about our operating environment. And that reality is that we live in an environment of low certainty and high ambiguity.

If you think you can sustain a profitable company without integrity, think Enron, think about the mortgage bankers who caused the 2008 financial collapse, or think about the businessman who bought $15 novelty golf ball detectors and sold them around the world as bomb detectors for $30,000 each and is now in prison for a long stretch. While these are extreme cases, we don't trust people who don't have integrity, by definition. I trust people who are honest, and people who have integrity are honest.

We operate in a highly competitive marketplace. If we do not improve, we will fail. Without integrity, we cannot face the real issues in our companies that are holding us back from growth and innovation. And if we don't face them honestly, we can't figure out how to fix them. I worked with a team whose management was continually concerned about their productivity. After spending just a little time with the team, it was clear to me that they were trying to operate with just a few old development servers, and that "overnight" builds were not complete until lunch the following day. The problem was not the attitude or professionalism of the team, but the procurement process that surrounded them. It was fixed in less than 24 hours.

Identifying and facing up to the real issues in the organization enables each of us to work toward solving, or at least mitigating, the real issues we are faced with.

If we are to build a collaborative, committed organization, everyone needs to avoid game playing or manipulation. If individuals or organizational processes do not act with honesty and integrity, it will become known. In this situation it is virtually impossible to build fully engaged teams who are committed to the business's success. The team's response to this behavior is to learn to play games in return, making it impossible to come to a joint reliable understanding of estimates or risks.

In Summary

An organization will be stable only if trust and ownership are in balance. The team is trusted and the team takes ownership. Command and control does work, but is far less effective than a high-trust, high-ownership organization.

To deliver maximum value, leaders must overcome their fear of failure and trust their teams. And they need to actively help their teams take ownership of the delivery rather than taking control and directing their teams on how to deliver.

The leader's initial assumptions about the team shape the team's behavior in line with the leader's assumptions. If the leader assumes the team cannot be trusted, then the team will not have ownership.

Moving up and to the right, to the green, will not happen automatically, but there are a set of simple behaviors and attitudes, detailed in this chapter, that will build ownership and commitment in the team. We'll cover how you move through the model in the next chapter.

In addition, teams must be aligned with the business goals of the organization. And everyone must deal and be allowed to deal honestly with ambiguity.

CHAPTER 3

BUILDING TRUST AND OWNERSHIP

The Big Ideas

- In the Trust-Ownership Model, the diagonal is stable but the lower-left quadrant (Command and Control) is incredibly limiting.
- Wherever you start, think of moving toward Energy and Innovation, the upper-right quadrant.

Getting to "Green"

So, how do we get to Energy and Innovation—the green?

Now we don't want to be judgmental, so if you are fortunate enough to have a team and an organization that are already well established in the green, no need to read further. If, on the other hand, you are like us, and need to move up and to the right, the first step is to figure out where you are. In this chapter, we provide a set of questions for you, as the leader, and a set of questions for your team to help you figure out where you are and where your team thinks they are. Next, we talk about how to move from where you are to where you want to be. Finally, we start the conversation about common obstacles you may encounter—we call them walls—and what you can do about them.

This chapter is about *how* you move toward the green. In our discussion we reference tools that will help you in this quest and provide details of all the tools in Chapters 4 through 9.

Let's start at the beginning—the assessment.

Trust-Ownership Assessment

The first step in moving toward a high-performance, innovative, motivated culture is recognizing—and being honest with yourself—where you are right now.

So how can you know where are you in the Trust-Ownership Model? (See Figure 3.1.)

As a leader, where do you think you and your team are? Where do you think your team thinks you are?

Let's look a little closer. And ask the team. The questions that follow can help you and the team to find out where you might be. It is always good to have the assessment done anonymously. Why? It is very difficult for leaders to admit they have a command and control style. They think they trust the team and the team won't take ownership—they are in the black quadrant, Failure. Conversely, it is difficult for the team to face the fact that they might have abdicated their ownership or never even tried to take it. They feel they are too controlled—they are in the red, Conflict.

We have included a sample assessment form in Appendix B, Trust-Ownership Assessment.

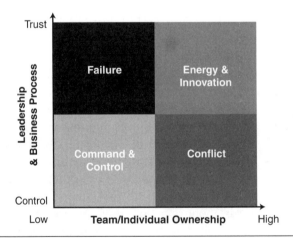

FIGURE 3.1 Trust-Ownership Model

Assessment Questions

We want to assess on Trust (the y-axis) and Ownership (the x-axis). Honestly dealing with ambiguity is part of Trust, and we have added questions to address this. Because teams cannot take ownership without knowing what they are taking ownership of, we have additional questions to address business alignment.

There are two sets of questions: one set for the team to answer and one set for the leader to answer.

Remember, we are dealing with perception and there are no right answers. In general, we want to get answers to questions and learn about where the team is in terms of ownership.

We want to know the answers to the following questions related to the team members:

- Do they feel trusted? Can they make decisions without being micromanaged?
- Do they have the latitude to deal with uncertainty?
- Do processes let them control important aspects of their lives such as how they do their work and how they organize their teams?
- Can they take risks without the fear of punishment?

To determine whether the teams have ownership for aligned results, we want to know whether teams

- Feel they can pursue different options to get to the goals.
- Can identify how what they do affects company results.
- Believe their work makes a meaningful difference in the lives of customers.

For leaders, the focus is slightly different.

On trust and ambiguity, we want to know how leaders answer the following questions:

- How comfortable are you giving guidance and letting your teams define the path they will take?
- How much experimentation do you allow?

- How frequently do you, in order to save time or avoid risks, tell your teams what to do and how to do it?
- Do you shield your teams from making commitments when there is still too much uncertainty?

On ownership and alignment, we want to know whether leaders

- Spend a significant portion of their time describing why the teams' work matters.
- Actively look for ways to reduce distractions so that teams can focus on delivering.
- Work every day to develop the skills, talents, and capabilities of their teams.
- Over time become less and less involved in how the teams operate.

To make it simpler for you to assess where you and your teams are in the Trust-Ownership Model, we have created the following questions (which are also available in Appendix B).

On a scale of 1 to 10, with 1 being the lowest and 10 being the highest, answer the following questions.

For the team on trust and ambiguity (the y-axis):

Low (1–3)	Medium (4–7)	High (8–10)
I have to get permission to do anything.	Managers and processes sometimes get in my way.	I am trusted to do my work.
I am told what to do and how to do it.	I can sometimes find my own solution.	I am trusted to always be able to find my own solution.
If I don't do things the approved way, I am at risk.	There are certain low-risk things I can do.	I can take chances without feeling at risk.
I always must give the organization exact numbers.	I sometimes can tell the organization when I am uncertain.	I can honestly tell the organization when I am uncertain without risk.

For the team on ownership and business alignment (the x-axis):

Low (1–3)	Medium (4–7)	High (8–10)
We are told how to do our work.	Our team can define parts of the solution.	Our team has full ownership of the solution.
I don't know what the goals are.	I understand some of the goals.	I clearly understand the organization's business goals.
What's a value proposition?	I think I understand some of the value proposition.	I clearly understand and agree to the value proposition for my project.
I'll only get something done if I know someone is going to ask me for it.	I feel responsible for small parts of the project.	I feel personally accountable for delivering on the organization goals.
I don't see how my work connects to organizational goals.	In some cases I can connect my work to organizational goals.	I can directly link my work to organizational purpose and goals.

For the leader on trust and ambiguity (the y-axis):

Low (1–3)	Medium (4–7)	High (8–10)
I trust no one on my team.	I trust some of my team.	I trust my entire team.
I require that everything must be defined before the team can do anything.	The big things, such as cost, schedule, and scope, must be defined before the team can do anything.	I honestly accept and allow genuine ambiguity and uncertainty from my team.
My team cannot take risks without my approval.	I let my teams take risks—but only when the risks are low.	I encourage my team to take risks in order to deliver value more effectively.

For the leader on ownership and business alignment (the x-axis):

Low (1–3)	Medium (4–7)	High (8–10)
It's my neck on the line. They better do what I tell them to do.	My team can solve some parts of the solution.	My team has ownership of the entire solution.
My team doesn't understand or accept the organization's goals.	My team understands some of the organization's goals.	My team understands and accepts the organization's business goals.
My team doesn't understand or accept the project's goals.	My team understands some of the project's goals.	My team understands and accepts the business goals of the project.
My team doesn't understand the value proposition at all.	My team gets the small picture, but I own the big picture.	My team understands and accepts the project's value proposition.

You need to collect the data in a nonthreatening way so you can get real information. Then average the scores. Look at the distribution and look for patterns.

Now take a look at where you and your team are in the model (refer to Figure 3.1).

Where does your team think they are? Where do you think they are? The most telling combination is the team's view of the trust they feel along with the leader's view of the ownership taken by the team.

Leaders may think they trust their team. However, the assessment will let them know if the team really does feel trusted. On the other hand, leaders may feel the team is not taking ownership, but the team may feel they are not allowed to take it.

Now that you know where you are, in the following sections we talk about how to move to the Energy and Innovation quadrant, into the green.

Getting to Trust and Ownership

The Trust-Ownership Model is an interesting, possibly enlightening, and highly nuanced way to look at the role of leaders, processes, individuals, and teams in getting to a high-performance culture that is focused on and generates measurable business value. As is the case with most 2×2 models, the goal is to move into the upper-right quadrant.

(As an aside, I sometimes wonder if our heads would explode if the desirable state in a 2×2 model were in the lower-left quadrant—perhaps we simply cannot think of that position as being the goal.)

From the assessment in the previous section, you know where you are and what you want to move toward. Before we start on how you make that move, there are some observations we want to share with you.

The upper-left (Failure) and lower-right (Conflict) quadrants are not, over the long term, sustainable for individuals or teams. If there is constant conflict, people will tend to opt out by either losing their feeling of ownership, leaving the team or organization, or being asked to leave the team or organization. If there is continual lack of ownership, results will shrink and those who can will leave for opportunities that provide more ownership, or everyone will be invited to find something else to do.

Most organizations settle or stabilize in the Command and Control quadrant. Yes, we are aware that command and control has been in place and successful for many years. Given its long history, some might think that command and control is a viable option. But, while it has been the common operating model and has "worked," it also seems that it is not the optimal operating model.

In a perfect command and control environment, an employee's job is to place a widget into the correct place and then repeat this activity—forever. We tell the employee how to do the work and expect they will not do much thinking beyond putting the widget in the correct place. But in a dynamic, highly competitive market, we want the employee to do much more than place the widget. We want the employee to identify how to improve the entire process. We want the employee to question everything—perhaps we don't even need the widget. For this to happen, we need the employee to think. However, command and control, at worst, discourages or, at best, severely limits independent thought. The more challenging the environment, the more command and control suboptimizes performance.

The history of the past decades is replete with "maverick" companies operating in the upper-right quadrant that have achieved amazing results. These include W. L. Gore (maker of Gore-Tex and an amazing array of high-performing products and divisions) and Semco (with its maverick CEO, Ricardo Semler). In rapidly changing environments and markets, the fundamental philosophy of command and control (the leader or the process knows everything and makes the majority of the decisions) renders it ineffective. We need to move diagonally from Command and Control to Energy and Innovation. In other words, to get to optimal performance we need to increase trust and help the team take ownership.

Because we all start at different places in the Trust-Ownership Model, let's explore how to move from anywhere to the Energy and Innovation quadrant.

Moving Out of Failure

The Failure state results from high leader trust and low team ownership. The leader believes the team, left to itself, will do the right things. But because the team doesn't know what the right things are or doesn't care about finding out what the right things are, it pursues its own interest. Some leaders (or, more likely, managers or whatever we want to call persons in some authority position) are disengaged from the purpose of the organization or somehow cannot communicate that to the team. The team doesn't understand the "why" or the "what." Or the team might not believe in the goals or thinks they are unachievable. These managers assume that the team will know what needs to be done and do it. The managers have abdicated essential elements of their role and created a vacuum. And because the team does not feel ownership for the results, the vacuum remains. A leader cannot just trust the team and walk away. He has to help the team take ownership. In Chapter 5, Ownership Tools, we introduce tools that leaders can use to improve ownership.

We believe it is extremely rare to move from Failure to Conflict. The manager would have to go from being disconnected to being controlling. At the same time, the team would suddenly begin to take ownership for results. This is very unlikely to happen in combination. That leaves us with two more likely moves. The preferred move is for the manager to become a leader and help the team take ownership by making sure the team understands the "why" and "what" of the organization, team, and project—while still operating in an environment of trust. It is also possible for the team to self-develop ownership by thinking through and understanding the "why" and "what" of their work, but this is rare. Most teams, once they have given up or not taken ownership, have reasons for doing so. A leader needs to understand how this happened or why it still exists. It could be they previously had a command and control type of boss or a boss who changed priorities every day so they gave up.

Some years ago, we worked with a team who operated in the Failure quadrant. They had weak product management and thus very little direction on the goals of their product. They did the best they could but did not feel any real ownership for the product sales or success. They did what they were told but were not told much, and so they did what they wanted. When we first met them, we challenged them on their approach. They responded with something of a *victim* mentality: We have no control over what is happening to us; if the company wants better results, the company will tell us what to do. We described to them tools like Purpose Alignment, the Business Value Model, the Four Questions, and the Billboard Test (all tools that we provide in Chapter 5) to help them see their customer's viewpoint and needs. We helped them understand the "why" from their customer's point of reference. We asked them to apply those tools to their product and to their work. Doing this created some energy on the team. The members of the team started thinking about their customers' lives and how their product could make those lives better. They started filtering their product features and functions and project plans through what would provide the most business value—and did this in the absence of any real input from someone in a position of authority. Over time, their product got better and sales went up. The sales team started working with them directly in order to influence the product. In parallel, their official authority figure got on board—at a minimum, he had to explain why the product was doing so much better. In this case, the team led the transition. In other cases, the leader will be the one who directs the team as to the "why" and "what."

It might also be case that the path from Failure to Energy and Innovation requires that the leader first exert more control in order to get to a more stable place in the Trust-Ownership Model. Wait, did you just read that correctly? In order to move toward trust and ownership you might have to reduce ownership or impose more control? Yes. If the current situation is trending toward Failure, you might first need to get things under control.

You might find that you need to reduce the chaos before you can accomplish anything. As a result, you might do detailed project reviews (a form of increased control). You might impose some processes (a form of increased control) in order to reduce mistakes. You might mandate certain standards (a form of increased control). Without this increased control, the chaos will continue or at least not be reduced fast enough that you can get to improvement. Without improvement, you will struggle getting to Energy and Innovation. As the team matures and takes ownership for results, you can decrease the controls you imposed.

Here is a quick, personal example that emphasizes this approach. I had been with the company in a non-IT role for about three months. In spite of my previous experience in various IT leadership roles, I wanted nothing to do with IT nor was that expected. But as the company went through its preliminary Sarbanes-Oxley (SOX)[1] audits, it was clear that the IT controls were lacking enough to put SOX compliance at risk. And for a publicly traded company, failing a SOX audit was close to the death penalty. The CFO and treasurer came to my office and asked me to "take one for the team" and take on the role of CIO to ensure that there would not be any issues with SOX compliance in six months when the official SOX audit hit. The CFO and treasurer had valid concerns because the IT team had already failed the preliminary audit.

I spent a couple of days assessing the IT situation and found an IT team that was in the Failure quadrant. The previous IT leader—who kept a role in IT, now as my critic—had pretty much abdicated any leadership in getting to SOX compliance. He did not know enough about effective IT controls and so had turned the project over to his staff. The members of his staff felt they were getting no direction on what needed to be done. They felt ownership for their individual operating processes, but SOX compliance was such a nebulous concept for them that they could not make headway on what needed to be done. As a result, nothing was being done. After they failed the preliminary audit, I would have expected the team to get together, identify the issues, discuss and agree to the solutions, and then do what needed to be done. In this case, failing the audit just seemed to confuse and depress everyone in the IT group.

With such a massive project on such a short timeline, I knew that the biggest danger was the current unstable situation—we had to start making progress and quickly. I would have loved to move the entire team and project to the upper-right quadrant immediately by increasing the ownership, but ownership of what? The team did not know enough to be owners. To get to ownership, I had to first inject more control and become a much more involved leader than the CIO I'd replaced. But how could I do this? I met with each person individually and had them walk me through their processes. Together, we compared their processes to a baseline set of IT

---

1. A law requiring top management to individually certify the accuracy of financial information.

best practices. I explained that we needed to move from their process to the best practice. In one case, they were using a unique method for moving changes from testing and into production. I required them to use a process based on the ITIL standard. In doing this, I was asking them to "turn off their brains" and comply with the best practices. I promised that not only would this approach ensure SOX compliance, it would make their lives better. They would gain time back in their lives by doing things in a best practices way. Right then, I needed them to adhere to the control I was imposing on them. I suppose in an effort to keep the new boss happy, they implemented the best practices and we breezed through the SOX audits. But to get there, we had to first get closer to that all-important diagonal by temporarily increasing leadership control.

Moving Out of Conflict

"This is ridiculous!" Janet was a senior executive leading a delivery team of 1,300 and her boss had just dropped his version of her goals for the year. His redlined version of the goals she had submitted removed all the leadership goals and added an extensive list of project measurements that he wanted her to report on every week. She was being treated as a manager of tasks, not as the leader of a delivery organization that was essential in defining and implementing the organization's strategy. The new goals left no room for innovation, idea generation, or continuous improvement. And the time required to collect the detailed project measurements would reduce the time her team would have to deliver. Janet was in the Conflict quadrant. Her boss wanted to define how Janet did her job. She felt ownership for the company objectives. How could Janet resolve this conflict? If her boss insisted on controlling where Janet felt ownership, she would likely leave the organization—and the organization would lose a talented leader. In spite of Janet's best efforts to work through the conflict— explaining her rationale for her approach, pointing out best practices, emphasizing how her boss could focus on more strategic needs by letting her own her results—her boss was insistent that she do things his way. In the end, Janet chose to avoid the frustration and left the company.

You can move from Conflict but it is a more nuanced move. The conflict exists because the team feels ownership but the manager wants to control their actions. This transition requires that the manager become a leader by trusting the team and relaxing the controls. It is highly unlikely that the team can make this transition by itself—the leader must change.

If the team owns the wrong things, the leader can exert more control as to the "why" and "what" but must then quickly move toward a culture of trust because if the conflict remains, either ownership will suffer or the conflict will be significant enough to drive people away.

We once worked with a leader who operated in a blame culture. If something went wrong, the company president wanted someone to blame. This blame culture generated many negative traits but, perhaps most important, reduced risk-taking and experimentation. People were more concerned about being wrong than they were with getting things right. The leader wanted to move from an environment of command and control (sometimes bordering on conflict) but recognized his inability to—at least quickly—change the blame culture. In order to move his team into the upper-right quadrant, he took the blame for any mistakes or missteps his teams made. When the president looked for a scapegoat, the leader accepted responsibility. The leader did this in order to move his team to Energy and Innovation, and it worked. To make this happen, the leader had to develop an immense stockpile of credibility with the rest of the organization—particularly the president. Obviously, if the leader was taking the blame for any mistakes, he had to make sure that mistakes were few and far between. He spent an incredible amount of time improving his team's delivery by creating a culture of trust and enabling ownership. And this approach worked so well that the president rethought his knee-jerk reactions and stopped looking for someone to blame.

What is missing when a team is in the Conflict quadrant? Trust from the leader and/or processes and an easing up of the leader's controls. To move the team from Conflict to Energy and Innovation, the leader starts by creating a culture of trust (a tool for this is provided in Chapter 4, Trust Tools). Then the leader must give up his control over the team and begin to relax or shield the team from all controls.

In many organizations, there are plenty of examples of controlling processes—processes that exhibit a complete lack of trust in the individual or team. These range from employee appraisal processes to status reporting to purchase approvals.

"What are you doing?" we asked a senior leader of a reasonably large organization (with annual revenues of over $400 million).

"I need to buy something for $3,999 and I have to fill out eight purchase orders."

"Why not just do one order?"

"I only can approve $499. Every purchase order of $500 or more has to go all the way up to the president. And that approval cycle takes a really long time. But I need this equipment as soon as possible."

"$500? Really? But you are responsible for an annual budget of $120 million."

"Still, the policy is what it is. So we have all become skilled at breaking our needs into $499 purchase orders."

This bothered us enough that we scheduled time with the company president.

"Dan," we started, "Why can your leaders only approve purchases of up to $499?"

"Purchasing was out of control. I had to do something to get it under control. I figured that if I personally approved any purchase of $500 or more, we would stop wasting so much money."

Dan showed us his purchase order inbox. It was stacked with purchase orders waiting for his approval.

"When you review these, do you understand the rationale for the purchase order?" we asked.

"Sometimes I do. Other times, I call the requesting manager and have him explain it to me."

"How much time of your time does it take to review and approve the requests?"

"I usually allocate Friday afternoons to work through whatever is in my stack," Dan answered. "That way, approving the purchase orders does not interrupt my week."

"How many purchase orders have you ever rejected?"

He thought for a moment. "None."

"Why, then, do you go through the exercise of reviewing them if you always approve them?"

"Well," he thought for a moment, "if I review everything, then people will only ask to purchase what they really need."

"Why don't you just hire people whose judgment you trust?"

Even though our question was a bit tongue-in-cheek, he paused, this time longer, and said, "You are right. I guess I really don't trust that, without my review, they will make good decisions."

"Can you trust your managers? Is there anyone, besides yourself, you can trust?"

This president changed his policy. He gave his staff departmental budgets and goals and let them manage inside what they owned. And, to his credit, not only did he change how he managed but also how he led—he started to focus much more on the direction of the company and less on approving purchase orders.

As this example highlights, it is really up to the leader to increase the trust and decrease the controls, whether that control comes from the leader or from the processes that the leader implements or controls. So if the team is to move from Conflict to Innovation and Energy, the leader is the person who can make that happen.

Recognize that even when leaders behave with visible honesty and integrity it will be some time for the team culture to become the same. Even a single instance of negative behavior can do real damage to this, and once the team believes that the leader or company is not to be trusted it can take a very long time to rebuild.

However, once a culture of openness, integrity, and honesty is in place it becomes self-sustaining. The motivation and energy generated are rewarding to the entire team and enable them to maximize their delivery of value to the business.

Take a minute and think about the processes in your organization. How many of them, in any way, show a lack of trust?

Moving Out of Command and Control

As mentioned previously, Command and Control is the typical model. The leader (or process) makes the decisions and everyone else complies. However stable and normal this is, it is suboptimal and becomes more harmful depending on the pace of change in the market and environment—and today the pace of change is accelerating.

In looking at the Trust-Ownership Model, the solution is obvious—increase both trust and ownership (see Figure 3.2). That sounds nice but it is a challenge, primarily because Command and Control is normal and accepted. To move up the diagonal requires that both the leader and the team change what they do.

This almost certainly requires behavior change and, as we all know, behavior change can be difficult. Those pesky humans have shown an amazing ability to be change averse. When it comes to changing behavior and culture, there is an incredible amount of uncertainty. We don't know how people will react to being given more ownership. We don't know how people will respond to our increased trust. We don't know whether they will embrace the changes or fight them. In other words, there is an incredible

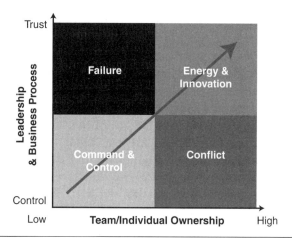

FIGURE 3.2 Move up the diagonal.

amount of uncertainty anytime we deal with those pesky humans. And, what is the current best way to deal with uncertainty? Use iterative methods!

Using the Trust-Ownership Model, we want to move our teams and organizations to the upper right. To make this move, we suggest doing it a step at a time with a pause after each step to learn and adapt.

What worked? What did not? What do we need to change as we take the next step toward trust and ownership?

For example, the move from Command and Control requires that the team begin to take ownership by making sure that they deliver on their commitments. Meeting a series of frequent commitments starts to build trust. Once the team has demonstrated the ability to follow through on their commitments, many enlightened command and control leaders will start to see the value and will move up the diagonal by trusting the team more. As the team gains trust from the leader, they take on more ownership and control shifts from the leader to them. The process is reinforced as each step of increased ownership is followed by delivery, which results in increased trust. A key aspect of this cycle is the delivery on commitments. If a team takes ownership and then commits to unreachable goals, the cycle will be broken and trust may actually regress.

Other leaders will be so entrenched in Command and Control that they cannot move. The team will try to take ownership but there will be resistance and the team will be in Conflict. In this situation the team must take more proactive steps in managing up (see Chapter 8, Tools to Deal with Walls). Managing up refers to the actions we take to manage the expectations and actions of those to whom we report. If the team reports to a micromanager, there are things the team can do to create some space and freedom from the oppression of Command and Control.

Likewise, the leader must get out of the business of making the small "how" decisions and focus on the big "what" and "why" decisions. This takes a leap of faith for both the leader and the team. From the leader's perspective, it was probably in part due to your decision-making track record that you are in a leadership position. You now have to walk away from something that led to your success and position.

The team must look for and take on more ownership and responsibility. The members of the team should individually and collectively look for decisions that they could and should own. This implies that they will ask and learn enough to understand the purpose of their work. If the leader is unwilling to give up that control, the situation moves toward conflict. But let's assume that is not the case—the leader develops trust and the team takes ownership. This creates a virtuous—but counterintuitive—cycle in which the leader's increasing trust is rewarded with better ownership and results and the team's ownership helps the leader fill the true role of a leader—setting the direction and vision and getting out of the business of making small decisions.

Please recognize that this might be uncharted waters for everyone—the leader, the team, the leader's leader, the team's peers, et cetera. That is why this book emphasizes tools that help not only the leader and team make this transition but also the operating culture of the organization. A trusting, owning culture is different from a command and control culture.

Uncharted waters exactly. And like all the hazards that come with such waters, combined with uncertain weather, the challenges and barriers will arrive.

Hitting the Walls

"Things are going okay. Why should we change?" Some people will like it the old way and won't want to change. Some people don't want to collaborate and won't. Here are more examples. You probably have more of your own.

- I need permission.
- Our leaders have to change first.
- It will never work in this culture.
- It's a fad—I can lie low and wait it out.
- It's not my job.
- We can't do this until we have shipped this release.
- There are non-collaborators here we can't work with.
- The process police.
- The organization requires waterfall processes.
- The organization won't accept uncertainty.
- I don't have anyone to replace the anti-bodies on my team.
- I'm too busy.
- People believe the leader is more interested in blame than in learning.
- People are not mature enough to take responsibility.
- People are comfortable not being accountable.

We call these walls, which you might encounter in your transition. Why do we call them walls? Because they stand between you and your team moving to the green.

There are many ways to deal with such walls: Go around them, create a door or window through them, tear them down completely, and remove them. What is most likely going to happen is you will be cruising along and bam! You've run right into a wall. We provide an entire chapter on the tools to help you (Chapter 8, Tools to Deal with Walls) but you have to provide your own first aid (sorry).

In Summary

We all want to move into the green, Energy and Innovation. But the movement can be difficult. First, assess where you are and where your team thinks you are. Then begin the movement toward the green using the tools provided in the next four chapters. And when you hit a wall? We have several tools to help in Chapter 8.

Remember, it is the leader who ultimately creates the Trust-Ownership culture.

CHAPTER 4

TRUST TOOLS

The Big Ideas

- You can't make people trust each other.
- However, you can create a culture where trust can be built and thrives.

Why Trust Matters

"This team needs a really good leader. They need you."

You've been asked to take over the leadership of a struggling team. The lack of trust within the team sticks out like a sore thumb. Your current team exudes trust and it has made quite a difference—morale and productivity are high; ideas and the information everyone needs to be successful flow freely; team members help each other without taking over. In other words, they are a cohesive, collaborative team that delivers results.

So how do you help your new, struggling team become a trusting team? This chapter is not about how people develop trust in their personal relationships. There are many articles written on that topic [4, 2]. Rather, this chapter addresses how leaders can create a culture where trust among team members is fostered, flourishes, and thrives—where people who have not begun to trust each other discover the possibility.

The first step is to assess whether you have broken trust in your team or it is just that they have yet to build trust with each other. Each of these situations has to be dealt with differently. Once the broken trust issue is resolved, focus on how to create a culture where trust within a team or with other teams can develop and thrive.

First, let's take a look at the price tags of not having trust in an organization.

Lack of Trust Price Tags

Why should you spend the effort in creating a culture of trust? Look at the transaction costs, the number of decisions and/or actions you make when interacting with someone or something. How long does it take you to get a task done by someone you don't trust? There is the preparation time as you figure out how to approach this person and how to clearly state your request. In the conversation, how many times did you say the same thing in different ways to ensure you were heard? How many times did you check to make sure that he correctly heard what you said? How often did you check to see if he will deliver what and when he said he would? The transaction costs of distrust are high. In a non-trusting environment, people spend a large amount of time protecting themselves. No wonder teams without trust exhibit low productivity.

However, there is data on the price tag to a company's bottom line when it lacks trust. The Great Place to Work Institute determines the 100 Great Places to Work every year for *Forbes* magazine. In their research of the candidates, they have developed what they call a Trust Index, and the companies are also ranked by this index. From 2004 to 2009, the top 100 trust companies generated revenue growth twice that of the second ranking 100 trust companies and four times the average of the S&P 500 [5].

Trust Assessment

What does a team without trust look like?

How do you know that a team lacks trust? Look for the following signs:

- **Fear**—People are hesitant to speak up—perhaps out of fear of failure or humiliation.
- **Secretive, territorial, everyone out for themselves**—Individuals on the team seem to pontificate and spout monologues and at the same time keep valuable information from the team.
- **Lack of engagement**—Team members do not appear to support each other and often don't participate in team discussions and decisions.

- **Defensive and negative**—People have closed body language; they hardly ever say a good word about other team members or the tasks at hand.
- **Judgmental and condescending**—Ideas are often dismissed without consideration or criticized unfairly.
- **Passive-aggressive behavior and lack of integrity**—In meetings, some people agree to one thing but outside the meetings say and do another.
- **Impatient, people are easily agitated**—Tension often appears in every working encounter; at the same time, people lack initiative and patience.
- **Gossip runs rampant, as does complaining**—Team members talk behind each other's backs, and most humor is mean-spirited instead of healthy, fun humor.

It is quite a challenge to take on such a team and lead them to trusting each other, especially when you are faced with the fact that as a leader, you cannot change people. You can't make people trust each other. Ordering people to trust each other just doesn't work.

Still, you want to take on the leadership of this team. You know many of the team members. They are a talented group and have produced great results on other teams. The project they are working on is important to the company, and you figure you can help. But there is one more question you need to consider.

One of the team members comes to you and asks, "Can I talk to you about one of my team members who is giving me trouble?"

"Sure." Then comes the first, important question, "Do you trust him?" And the usual reply? "No." That's an issue. People know when you don't trust them. They *really* know when their *leaders* don't trust them. As Ricardo Semler asks in his book, *The Seven-Day Weekend* [6], if you don't trust the people on your team, why are they on your team? For that matter, why are they in your organization?

Before you make a decision about leading this team, ask yourself one final question: "Can I trust everyone on this team?" You may not know all of them well, but you must make sure there is no one on the team you distrust.

Your answer to this question is yes, so you accept the leadership role for this team. Now what do you do?

Broken Trust or Lack of Trust

"What do you do when there is one person on a team that no one trusts?" "Are you sure they don't trust him?" Our answer is, "Is it a lack of trust or has trust been broken?"

Broken trust is like a cut rope. There are many strands wound together that give the rope its strength. Once cut, repairing the rope requires matching each piece, strand for strand. Not only does it take time, but the rope will never be the same and will not have the strength the original rope had. Can a distrusted person repair his relationship with the rest of the team? Does he want to? Does the team want to rebuild the relationship with him? And does he have the skills to do so? Possibly, but the time and effort to do so is very high, and the results might not be optimal or even acceptable.

However, there may be no broken trust in the team, just lack of trust. If so, the trust can be developed. You need to find out if trust is broken or not yet developed. Take the time to make some observations and assessments to see how deep the distrust might be and identify some possible causes.

Interview each team member in confidence. Ask about how they like their work on the team, what's working and what's not. If they could fix what's not working, what would they do and why? Ask what obstacles are getting in the way of their individual success and their team's success. Do they feel like the team can deliver the expected results? And if not, what can be done to improve their chances? Check to see if they feel the right people are on the team, that everyone has the knowledge, experience, and commitment to complete the project. Most important, ask if they trust everyone on their team. They may be uncomfortable answering such direct questions with their new leader. Listen for the ring of truth in what people say and make note of what they leave out of your conversation.

Walk the floor. Watch and listen to how the team works. Is one person talking all the time? Are people ignoring one or more of their fellow team members? Are there consistent put-downs or constant dismissals of one person's ideas? Spend time in the break room. How do they interact there? Do they avoid someone? Do they talk about ideas? Do they avoid eye contact with some of their team members? Listen to the interactions within the team and with people outside the team, and look at their results and progress.

Look for trends or threads in your conversations and observations. Did you sense any red flags or unauthentic answers? Did one name come up again and again as someone who did not deliver as he said he would? Did one person consistently withhold information? Was he constantly noted as hard to get along with, never listening, saying one thing and doing another? The issue of distrust seems to point to one person and a hard decision faces you. Your decision will not only affect the relationship between the individual and the team but will also shape the team's view of you.

You have two choices: Keep this person involved with the team at some level or remove him. What is your first response? Your intuitive answer may be the right one, but before you act, answer a few more questions. How valuable is he to your team, to your project? Can your team succeed without him? What are the negative impacts if he leaves? Or if he stays?

Apply the "vacation test." See how the team does when the problem team member goes on vacation for a few days. Take this person off the team and give him something else to do. Place him where he cannot interfere with the day-to-day functions of the team. What happens to the team productivity, their motivation, their morale?

If you come to the conclusion that the team benefits from his removal, then make the move as soon as possible. But what if you need to keep him involved with the team at some level? Then what do you do?

Again you have two choices: Ask the team to integrate this person in some way into the project, or create a one-person island inside the team. With the trust problem on the island, members of the team interact via some prescribed methods in order to keep communication to the bare minimum necessary to get the job done. Both integration and the island are difficult to implement and will take time and effort to accomplish. Help the team take ownership of the issue. Sit with the team without this person and ask them how they can work with him. What team norms would have to be established to make it happen? What would they need to be successful with him on the team? What do you need from you to make it happen? What does the team want you to do when the disruptive person interferes too much with the other team members? Come to an understanding that, while the team must work with this disruptive person, they do not have to view him as a team member. They can collaborate without him. They must make decisions with this person only when it involves his work.

Everyone must understand that sabotaging the disruptive person is not acceptable and would be sabotaging the team's own efforts. Ensure that the team will be measured as a team, not as individuals. While they can't control the disruptive person in their midst, they can use his knowledge and experience to succeed as a team.

You have resolved the situation with the difficult person, but are your team issues now solved? Do you have a trusting, productive team? Not quite! They now have to build trust.

Creating a Culture of Trust

How do you create a culture of trust?

"Just pick people who are trustworthy." I get this answer at times from my colleagues.

"And how often do leaders actually get to do that?" I ask.

Think how nice it would be. You are assigned a project. You pick people you know are good, competent, and trustworthy. You give them responsibility to deliver within the constraints and they become a trusting, high-performance team. All within 15 minutes. You may have the opportunity to have this experience once in your lifetime—but probably not. Realistically, like it or not, you are given your team members with all their foibles, shared history, and excess baggage.

As the leader, your role, style, and behavior will lay the groundwork for building a culture of trust.

To start, there are a few things *you* need to pay special attention to about *you*. Authenticity is essential—your team will see right through you if you are not authentic (missing your own ring of truth), and their lack of trust will continue. Be trustworthy and own up to your own foibles, history, and mistakes. Share all information with the team and when you can't, tell them why. You have to show you trust your team—first.

Give up command and control leadership and don't micromanage. Telling people what to do and how to do it shows a lack of trust. If you trust people, you believe they will do what they say they will do and they know best how to do it. Micromanagement sends a message that you do not trust those you are leading.

Trust me—your leadership will be tested by your team. Team members will come back several times to see if you will rescue them, fix it for them, tell them what to do and how to do it, if you will really accept mistakes, and whether you genuinely trust them to deliver. They will watch carefully and test your trustworthiness. Will you listen? Will you give them the information they ask for? Will you admit your mistakes? Will you be honest?

Now focus on creating a culture where the team can build trust among themselves.

So what can you, as the leader, do? Use any of the following techniques, either one or as many as you need:

- Remove debilitating fear.
- Use team-based measurements.
- Ask for small deliverables in short iterations.
- Expect success, allow mistakes.
- Take the fun out of being dysfunctional.

Let's take a closer look at each of these techniques.

Remove Debilitating Fear

Debilitating fear is what keeps team members from expressing their questions, solutions, analyses, and investigations. They are afraid of failure, humiliation, ridicule, loss of respect, and—the deepest fear—loss of their position, pay, and perhaps their job. Fear results in paralysis and catastrophizing (making things seem worse than they are). They focus on avoiding mistakes rather than on delivering exceptional value.

I once worked for a nonprofit where people were always worried about their job security. When the issue came up, I asked them to figure out ways to solve that problem. They filled three easel-size sheets of paper with ideas and because they were their ideas, they implemented them. One great way to remove the fear is to ask the team how they want to do it.

Do you know what your team fears? Ask them. Get some sticky notes and pens, ask each person to write what their fears are in the team, one idea on each sticky note, as many ideas as they want. Have each person put their notes on the wall and ask the team to group them. Let each person vote on their biggest fears. Then break them into teams and have them work on solutions.

In his book, *Beyond Bureaucracy* [1], Warren Bennis states that in a collaborative environment (like a team) people fear three things: losing their identity; losing their intellectual mastery; and losing their individualism. Because each person is different, a leader must get to know each team member to learn how to remove these fears. I ask people questions to get to know them, something about how they think and why they are who they are. For example, "What was a major turning point in your life?" or "What was a book that made a difference in your life?" or "How do you define integrity?" I want to know something about the individual that might have formed his or her life in some way. This can give me some insight into how to address these fears of loss.

Some tools that can help are holding "lunch and learns" for team members to share their knowledge, having innovation days to try new things and demonstrate them, or asking experts to mentor team members and recognize efforts within the team.

Use Team-based Measurements

Measuring individual performance is a deterrent to collaboration and teams working together. Often, if individuals are measured on their own performance, they don't care how well the rest of the team does—they'll look out for themselves first. To change this dynamic, measure the team, not the individuals. This motivates the team to work together and help each other deliver a team success. You might not get your HR department to go along with this, but you can ask the team to evaluate themselves as a team. The key here is that they do not need to share this with anyone outside the team unless they want to. One executive who did this said it was the largest significant decision he ever made—that it made a great impact on the team toward improving their performance.

Ask for Small Deliverables in Short Iterations

Ask the team for rapid, incremental deliveries—small successes where they can see progress and successful results as a team. Let them make decisions on how they will do this, how they will do their own work, and how they will work together. They don't need you to tell them. Step back and let the team decide.

Expect Success, Accept Mistakes

Stress the motto "Fail early, fail fast." People learn from their mistakes. Right now, your team may be worried about taking a risk and failing. Sure, removing disruptive fear might help. Most important is your protecting them *and* your organization. Create a way for the team to fail safely. What does that mean? First, you don't want them to be embarrassed in front of your customers, in front of organizational leaders, and in front of other teams. Add a step in the processes (or better still, suggest they evaluate adding a step) where they can walk through their results before they go outside their team.

Remember, people learn from mistakes. Focus on the learning and not the mistake. This includes not allowing any judgments on ideas. All thoughts are accepted as something to discuss and look at as possibilities. If the team struggles with this, call them out on it.

Take the Fun Out of Being Dysfunctional

Ignore unprofessional behavior. What do you do about those who are gaming the system where team members leverage the leader to discredit a team member? This does not exist in a healthy team—one that is collaborative, understands and respects each other's contributions, remains focused, and has ownership. But you don't have that—yet. To get there, take the fun out of dysfunctional. Remove the reward people are getting for playing games within the team. When someone causes distractions, such as asking rhetorical questions with no real purpose—where they are trying to impress you with the right answer or embarrass you if you made a mistake—ignore this behavior. Stand quietly and do not say a word. Or look to others in the room and change the subject. Remember, negative attention can be a reward for many people.

Your Leadership Role

The team's efforts to build trust will have their ups and downs. There are a few things you can do to help that process move forward.

- **Be Authentic.** If the team feels you are not authentic, they will chew you up and spit you out. They need to know that your agenda is their success—that you are not putting your personal agenda over the purpose of the team and the organization.
- **Create Transparency.** Share all you can to help the team succeed, including understanding of the wider business needs and the big

picture. There are things you cannot share, so when information must be withheld, explain why.

- **Show Trustworthiness.** The team needs to know they can count on you.
- **Protect the Team Boundaries.** Be your team's advocate—go to bat for them, get the team what they need to succeed, and don't let the distractions of corporate bureaucracy and politics creep into their work environment.
- **Stay Positive.** The team will need acknowledgment, feedback, and recognition. Affirm what is working. Don't dwell on past failures or anything that could possibly be interpreted as judgmental. Negative feedback will be blown out of proportion, and its effects may take a long time to repair.

To help with this, remember Peter Drucker's advice to focus on a person's strengths rather than their weaknesses [3].

I once was giving a presentation. A person in the audience asked how leaders can be authentic and positive at the same time. I was speechless—for a moment. My reply was: If you can't find something positive to say, don't say anything. However, if you can't find something positive to say to your team, they will know this and will never respect you as a leader.

Making a Change

Remember, people are different. There may be some individuals within the team that may never trust the organization or its leader. Sometimes the only solution is for the individual to leave.

Some years ago I discovered a highly negative individual on one of my teams. Due to some previous history that I could not discover, he saw the organization and all of its leaders, including myself, as completely untrustworthy. He was very outspoken and was really damaging the motivation of the individuals he worked with.

Professionally he was a highly effective programmer, and so I spent some time trying to coach him and change his viewpoint. After a while it became clear that he was not going to change his views, and I felt that this was a situation that was bad for all of us. His negative attitude was infecting the team and their morale was falling. In discussions about problems and potential actions, he was always arguing strongly for the most conservative, risk-free, and low-productivity option.

In a deliberately nonconfrontational way I pointed out to him that he was clearly very unhappy working for the company and that it must be painful spending 8 or 9 hours a day working for people he didn't trust. I asked him why, if it was so painful, he didn't leave the company.

He did get a new job elsewhere and some months later contacted me to thank me for helping him move. He said it was something that he should have done much earlier.

His move was good for all of us. If you don't take care of a negative person or situation, the negativity will spread and the team will resent your not taking action.

Decision Filters

Use decision filters. These are questions that help each of us remain focused. When it comes to building a culture of trust, my decision filters are

- Will this help remove the fear of collaboration?
- Does this show the team I trust them?
- Will this show the team I am trustworthy and authentic?
- Does this show the team I expect success and accept mistakes?
- Will this help the team understand their purpose?

When you encounter almost any situation, you can ask these questions and decide how you can increase the trust between you and the team, among the members of the team, and between the team and everyone else.

Will blaming the team for missing a critical requirement show the team that you trust them? Probably not. So find a way to help them learn without blame.

Will admitting that you made a mistake when you gave your team the wrong budget figures show that you are trustworthy and authentic? It can't hurt. So admit your mistakes.

In Summary

Teams deliver great results when they take ownership. After working with a team on setting goals and objectives, leaders must step back and let the team work. You can't do this without trust—it is essential in engaging teams, retaining talent, fostering innovation, creating great working environments, and delivering results. When the trust goes out of a team, what can a leader do?

Hard as it may be, you must decide what to do when one member of the team has broken trust with the others. It really does not matter how it happened. To keep such a person on your team is costly. You must decide if it is better to take the person off the team or not. If you keep that person, you and the team must decide how to work with that person.

As the leader, make sure you trust or can build trust with everyone on your team. Be transparent and show you are open to new ideas and different ways of thinking. Practice collaborative leadership—give up micromanagement and command and control.

Leaders cannot make people trust each other, but they can create a culture that encourages trust and where trust flourishes and thrives.

References

[1] Bennis, Warren. *Beyond Bureaucracy: Essays on the Development and Evolution of Human Organization*. San Francisco: Jossey-Bass, 1993.

[2] Benson-Armer, Richard, and Stickel, Darryl. "Successful Team Leadership Is Built on Trust." *Ivey Business Journal,* May/June 2000.

[3] Drucker, Peter. *The Practice of Management*. New York: HarperCollins, 1954.

[4] Hurley, Robert F. "The Decision to Trust." *Harvard Business Review*, September 2006.

[5] Lyman, Amy. "The Trust Bounce." *Great Place to Work® Institute*, 2009.

[6] Semler, Ricardo. *The Seven-Day Weekend: Changing the Way Work Works*. New York: Portfolio, 2004.

CHAPTER 5

OWNERSHIP TOOLS

The Big Ideas

- If you provide the answers, you have taken ownership away from the team to find their own solution.
- Ownership cannot be given. Leaders need to help their teams take ownership.
- Leaders, focus is on "what" and "why" but never "how."
- The Macro-Leadership Cube is very useful in defining leader and team ownership.

Give or Take?

I remember my first major leadership job. I sat in my office for several days waiting for someone to come and tell me who I should go visit, what I should take on, and what needed to happen. Suddenly I realized no one was going to tell me! I had an area of responsibility with specific goals, and it was up to me to decide how to achieve them.

We have seen it many times. Most teams have never had ownership. When a leader walks in and says, "I trust you. You now have ownership," teams often don't know what to do and don't believe they really have ownership. If they don't understand the real goals of the business, they might go off and build something that does not align with the business goals or meet customer needs.

I asked several leaders I know how they help their teams take ownership. One thought for a minute and said it was difficult. Then he asked me how I did it. "Well," I said, "I try one thing and if that doesn't work, try another." "Exactly. It depends on the person."

In this chapter, we present ownership tools in three groups:

- How to keep us, the leader, from taking ownership away from our team.
- A collection of ideas for leaders to help their team take ownership.
- A Macro-Leadership Cube that helps define the constraints and enables the team to move anywhere as long as they stay inside the cube.

Let's take a look.

Taking Ownership

Ownership has many facets. Leaders can't give ownership; teams must take it. But they need help. In most cultures, teams are deep into "just doing what they are told" and are afraid to do anything else. So leaders must step back and help teams take ownership. Leaders can, however, block teams from taking ownership through control.

Unfortunately, it is very easy for leaders to take away ownership. It can happen in an instant. It is difficult not to take away ownership. In fact, often we have no idea we are doing it when we do it.

In this section, we provide tools for both efforts: helping our teams take ownership and then keeping ourselves from taking it back. Let's look at the easiest tool first.

Don't Take Away Ownership

"I'm stuck. I can't figure this out." We hear this many times from our team members. And our immediate response? "Have you tried ___?"

We are natural problem solvers and we want to help by finding the solution. However, when you do this, you take ownership away from this person or team. You now own the solution.

In many IBM teams, the architects used to approve designers' designs. Once they approved them, however, the architects owned the solution and if there were problems, the designers were off the hook—it wasn't their problem, it was the architects' problem. When this happened, the designers would set about building the approved solution. If it became apparent at any time that the approved design would not work, the designers thought, "It's not my fault. It will work eventually. Bob approved it!" They kept working on a flawed design, wasting many hours.

No longer. Architects make themselves available all day to discuss with designers what they have in mind. The designers are fully responsible and accountable. The architects never approve any designs, either formally or informally.

Don't Give Answers—Ask Questions

Our position in the company matters to some people. That means if you are a leader, subject matter expert, or thought leader, with lots of experience or many years with the company, people give your answer more weight and give their own answer less weight.

It is very easy for leaders to take away ownership by accident. One day one of my development leads stopped me in the hall and laid into me.

"This is just stupid. Why are you making us do it this way?"

I was completely taken aback and asked him what he was talking about.

"We've been told that you said we have to design the solution this way!"

Then I realized what had happened. We were all at the water cooler one day discussing potential solutions to this problem. I had simply said, "Would this work?" Because I was the senior manager, someone had taken my water cooler remark as a directive and decided that I was telling them this was the way the problem had to be solved. I quickly sorted this out but learned that it is incredibly easy to take ownership away from the team.

How do we not take ownership away from our teams? One way is to not give them the answers, no matter how hard they try to get one from you. Sound simple? Yes. However, it is not easy to do. To test this, find a peer you trust. Ask her to think up a problem that you could answer and have her work very hard to get you to give her the answer. You, on the other hand, will work very hard to not give her the answer but help guide her to discover the answer herself. Be careful you don't give the answer away in the questions you ask.

How did it go? Most managers find this very difficult. It is hard not to give the answer, especially if you *think* you know the answer. (Remember, times have changed. Your answer may not be the best answer these days.) Pollyanna asks, "How do you want to solve it?" And Niel asks, "What do you want me to do?"

Here are some questions other leaders have found useful in helping their teams:

- What problem are you trying to solve? What are your assumptions?
- How would you describe the issue?
- What options have you explored and why? What are the pros and cons? What solutions have you excluded and why? Is there anything that has not been considered so far?
- Who have you discussed this with? Do you know anyone who has done this before? What have others done to solve this?
- What is limiting your progress at this point?
- Which constraint could we relax?
- What feels right to you? What ideas do you have?
- Reasonable next step? What do you think should be done? What do you need to determine the solution? Do you need a stakeholder view?
- What would be best for our customer?
- How are you going to get more data?
- What will happen if you don't address the problem?

What questions work for you?

This takes practice. Write your best question on a sticky note and put it in a place to remind you all the time of what to say. And when you do blunder, apologize immediately.

Don't Leverage Your Position to Get What You Want to Hear

In what other ways do we take away ownership—unknowingly? Let's take a look at another example.

What happens when you get estimates from your team? "How long will it take you to build this?" the manager asks. "Three weeks," comes back the reply. And what's the first thing out of the manager's mouth? "Can you do it in less?" And because the manager is the boss and the developer might worry about his job or position and doesn't want to seem unhelpful, he says, "Okay, two weeks." Now who has ownership? The boss. Is the developer going to spend late nights getting it done? Not likely. Most people, when they are asked for something and commit to it themselves, will do all they can to make it happen, because they have ownership.

When Paul retired from IBM, he worked with us inside IBM as a consultant. One day we were in a conference room with our client taking a break. "Pollyanna," Paul asked, "how do I get reimbursed for my expenses? Do you have a form?" "No," I answered. "Give me an amount and we pay you." "No receipts?" "No, I don't want you wasting your time filling out forms or collecting receipts. Give me a number." Our client shook her head thinking about all the forms she had to fill out, all the corrections she had to make, all the receipts she had to justify. She didn't have ownership of company expenditures.

Don't Correct Mistakes—Ask Questions

In another example, I went for a set of X-rays one day. (I'm okay. Don't worry.) My doctor had ordered a set they did not do very often, and the technician was training someone new. She asked if I minded her showing the new technician how it worked. "No problem," I said. After showing him how to do it, I let them practice on me. Then, one X-ray had to be repeated. "Let the trainee do it this time," I suggested. She agreed. But she kept correcting him through the entire process. She took away ownership and his chance to really learn how to do the X-ray. All she needed to do was ask him to try again. Then he would try harder until he got it right.

Once, a CEO of a billion dollar company was shocked at my direction to not correct people. "What if my accountant comes in and I spot an error? Why can't I tell him the answer?" he pleaded. "Well," I said, "if you do, next time he won't spend the extra effort to make it right. He will let you correct it. You have ownership." He never forgot that conversation. Whenever we talked, he gave me his report, "I have not been correcting others' errors. I ask them to check their work and make sure it is right before they give it to me."

Help Teams Take Ownership

We were building a control system for an electrical power plant. The team had identified all the efforts and each person had volunteered for what they would deliver. The very next day, Jeff appeared at my desk. He had assumed responsibility for a key piece.

"Hi, Jeff. What do you need?" I said.

"Pollyanna, how do you want me to build this?"

"Well, build it the way you want."

The next day, he was back at my desk. "Pollyanna, how do you want me to design this?"

"Whatever you think."

The next day, he was again at my desk. "Pollyanna, how do you want me to do this?"

I was speechless. After a moment I said, "Jeff, you are here because of your ability, expertise, and commitment. Give it your best shot. I am here if you need me."

So off he went. Then I was stuck. I couldn't check up on him—that would have shown I didn't trust him. So I waited it out. I saw he was interacting often with the team but he never came back to me. As we began integrating the designs and pieces together, his work required the least effort and had the fewest problems. He had taken ownership.

You can't give people ownership. You can trust them and provide the goal and hope they take ownership, but you can't walk away. Most people are so ingrained in the "just tell me what to do and how to do it" culture, they may not even know how to take ownership.

Let's look at another example.

Independent performance reviews not only take away ownership of our evaluating our own goals, but stack ranking of those reviews also drastically reduces collaboration and teamwork. It seems that people think, "Why should I help Dan? If he ranks higher than me, he will get a bigger raise." This is so counterproductive.

"We need our VP to get HR to stop these reviews. It is getting in the way of our being productive as a team," Tony said at a recent meeting.

"Hmm," I started to think. "We could ask for a minor change. We could try to understand why they need us to do reviews and find an alternative. We could . . . ." Then I stopped. I was taking ownership away from HR.

"We need to find some people in HR who will listen," I started, "and show them the Trust-Ownership Model. After explaining how it works and how performance reviews get in the way, we ask for their help in getting us to the green box."

We explained the issue to the HR department and let them take ownership of improving the performance of the teams in their organization—the entire organization.

How can leaders help teams and people take ownership? It cannot be done without the team feeling they are trusted. That must be clear from you and clear to them. Let's look at some tools for building this trust.

Create a Safe Place to Fail

We worked with an architecture firm with seven executives and over 100 architects. Every design put in front of a client had to first be approved by the one of the seven executives. This created quite a bottleneck. "It's our reputation," the executives explained. "It has to meet our standards or we are sunk." That's a good reason but it was really slowing them down in delivering to their customers. In addition, the 100 architects felt stifled. Even worse, they felt little ownership for their work product. Their attitude was, "It does not matter if I do great work—the executives will find something they don't like." So we created a process where the architect would present his design to the company before it went to the customer. Anyone could attend and make comments, including the executives. And because the review was in an open forum, it provided a safe place for the architect to "fail" and then correct before his design was presented to the customer.

Find a way for teams to test out their ideas before failing in public.

Let the Team Make Decisions

I can't think of a single decision I should make for my teams. I am technologically dead. All I do is implement the decisions the team makes. Okay, I ask questions—to understand why they want to do what they want to do. I ask about how that helps them deliver the product but actually I have no clue if it is right or wrong. I have found that if I treat people as professionals, they act as professionals.

Recently, a colleague was talking about a team he was working with. Everyone was complaining about who didn't do what and all the cliques that had formed in the team. It went on for hours. Tough. Someone was treating them as kids—and had not let them take ownership. They could not make any decisions about how to deliver and waited for someone to tell them.

A good question to ask teams is, "When you make a decision, are there any impacts on the business or on the customer?" Be sure there is no hint of judgment in your delivery.

If the team struggles with reaching a decision, introduce the collaboration process where they brainstorm using sticky notes, then group and prioritize them. This process is detailed in Appendix C, Collaboration Process.

Trust First and Be Trustworthy

"Suspicion is a permanent condition." [1]

If a team doesn't feel trusted, they won't be able to take ownership. Why should they? If the team is not yet used to ownership or trust they might not believe that they have ownership. You will be tested—again and again. They will try to get you to take ownership. This is not because they don't want to have ownership; they just may not be used to it or they don't know how to take it. And they may not know the boundaries of their ownership. This is where the Macro-Leadership Cube (described later in this chapter) comes into play. Set the boundaries of the cube together with your team.

Trust first! Think of someone you are not sure you can trust. How long is it going to take for that person to prove to you that he is trustworthy? Too long. But if you start by assuming everyone is trustworthy, you generate the results of a culture of trust immediately. Rather than not trusting people until they prove trustworthy, trust them until they prove they cannot be trusted.

Sell the Vision

If the team is to take ownership it needs a clear understanding of the goals and business factors associated with the project:

- Spend time with the team exploring and elaborating on the high-level goals of the project and the current business and market conditions.
- When building the vision be careful not to get into too much detail. Focus on what drives value by sticking to higher-level stories, situations, and scenarios. This should keep you out of defining how the team is to do the work. If you are defining features and functions rather than results, you are at the wrong level.
- When you review their work with the team, give clear feedback on their progress toward the desired results and, again, avoid the "hows" of their methods. Include information about the state of the market and the competition.

Connect the Team with Customers

Make contact with key potential customers and users, and help the team work with them to prioritize features and functions to be delivered. Make sure customers are involved with the team throughout their project.

When moving to iterative methods, IBM implemented a way for teams to securely provide customers with intermediate versions of their products. They also created a forum so that customers could give feedback directly to the development teams. As you might suspect, there was more than a little anxiety about directly connecting customers to software engineers! For the first IBM project delivered this way, the results were outstanding: New, market-leading capabilities were added during the development cycle, and the number of customer questions after shipment was dramatically lower. Most of the potential issues were resolved during product development.

Enable the Team

There are many ways to enable the team, and we want it be in the broadest possible way. Look to what they need and try to provide it. Look for inhibitors and try to remove them. Search for common underlying themes in the retrospectives or in issues that arise and try to address them. Be proactive.

Build the Team

Ensure the team is skilled and staffed well enough to deliver. Even if your resources are constrained you can always find ways to get more capacity and capability from the team—not by browbeating or intimidation but by moving them toward Energy and Innovation. If the team feels that some individuals are not suited to the team, help those individuals move on.

Equip the Team

Make sure they have everything they need to succeed. Compared to the costs of experienced employees, any tools, software or hardware that help them succeed and improve are a great investment. Be aware that sometimes teams will live with a bad situation because they are used to it, and used to the organization refusing any requests.

Support the Team

Build an infrastructure that *supports* the team. Find ways to limit non-customer-value work done by the team. Shield them from time and capacity wasters.

Other Ownership Tools

Talk about ownership with the team. Pure openness about your trust and faith in the team's ability to deliver great things could be enough. Let them know you aren't abandoning them. Explain to them that you will be available for times when they get "stuck," but they are now the owners. During this discussion bring up prior examples of how individuals and the team have stepped up when it was required. Remind them of their positive actions during those times. Make comparisons between prior successes and the new ownership you are asking them to take on. Let them know you've "got their backs."

Let the team work their way out of a particular problem. Going through trial and error and any resulting failures is critical in experiential learning. Provide the team with confirmation that you know they are taking a risk and that you are backing their effort 100 percent. Once they have solved the problem you can let them know they have taken ownership and have ownership from that point forward.

Use the "vacation method" on yourself. Let the team know you will be "out" for at least two to three weeks and not available for phone or e-mail contact. It might be a good time to take that trip to Fiji that you've always dreamed about. If you are willing to disconnect yourself from the project, the team will realize they must step up and take ownership. Upon your return from vacation, do not return to the "old way" of doing things. Recognize and reward the Team for their progress and keep the momentum going.

Another tool to use is to take on a new and different responsibility for yourself. Explain to the team your new duties and let them know you will not be able to spend as much time with them, but of course you trust them and know they will do a great job. Ultimately, you want to work yourself out of the job of running the team.

As you and the team mature, you can let them take on the biggest trust/ownership move of them all: Let the team know *they* are responsible for divvying up the year-end bonus, including *yours*. If your company has given you complete budget responsibility, see if the team will take the ultimate step of running themselves like their own small business.

Work with the team to minimize the amount of oversight. Limit the metrics gathered to measures that give an overall view of project progress and quality and provide really useful information for the team. There is a longer discussion on metrics in Chapter 9, Metrics, but for now focus on minimizing the cost of collection and reporting and maximizing the value to the team.

Macro-Leadership Cube

I once managed a nightmare systems implementation project to a very successful conclusion. In this project, I applied everything I had ever learned—and learned new things—just to deliver a highly constrained project in a rapidly changing environment. I felt as if I was at the very top of my project management game. In order to not let this newly found knowledge go to waste, I decided to train the project managers on my staff in all of the methods I has just used to pull off this project management miracle. I spent weeks documenting the details of the tools and approaches. Then I turned this document into a comprehensive training program and scheduled the first of what I expected would be several training programs. The night before the first session, I reviewed my 70-page treatise on highly effective project management. It was a thing of beauty. It described, in an almost minute-by-minute schedule, how a project manager should conduct the day, the week, the project. If a project manager followed my template, project success was nearly guaranteed.

As I finished my review, a troubling thought hit me. I had, in a mere 70 pages, described exactly how I thought someone should manage a project. But that was just me. Was I, by taking this approach, becoming a project management micromanager? The foundation of my 70 pages was certainly the belief that I knew better than anyone else. Did I? To be sure, I was pretty good but did I know it all? And by prescribing it all, was I limiting motivation, freedom, and innovation? I paused and thought through my approach again. What did I really want to accomplish? I wanted my project managers to not only be successful but also to have ownership for their work and to innovate and share their practices. I wanted them to love their work. Would or could they if I handcuffed them to my methods?

So I started over. I reviewed my 70-page masterpiece but this time looked for project management principles—principles that I found important and that might be helpful to someone else. Instead of laying out a detailed communication schedule and protocol, the important principle might be, "In the absence of communication, people assume the worst. Avoid this with frequent, meaningful communication." No longer did I define what "frequent" and "meaningful" meant. That was up to the project manager and his project team and stakeholders. In the course of the next hour, I reduced my 70 pages of project management excellence to half a page of project management principles. The next day, I walked the project managers through these principles and gave them some examples. That was it. They now knew what I considered to be important, but how they applied these principles was entirely up to them.

To keep myself from ever becoming a micromanager, I have developed and use a simple graphical device. This device is a bit hokey, but it helps keep me on track. I call it the Macro-Leadership Cube (see Figure 5.1) to contrast it with micromanagement. The idea is that, as a leader, I should focus my attention on the "what" and the "why" of our tasks, projects, and processes but never the "how." Visually, the "what" and the "why" form the walls of a cube.

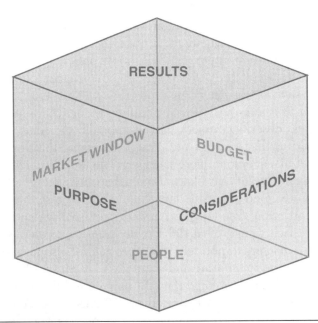

FIGURE 5.1 Macro-Leadership Cube

These walls can include the Purpose and goals of the project, the expected Results, the available Resources, the targeted Time-to-Market, any Standards that apply, the Budget, et cetera—anything that defines the "what" and the "why" as well as any constraints that might impact the project. However, because they are so important, the Results *must* be one side of the cube and the Results must be qualified—that is, specific. We once worked with a nonprofit that lobbied their senators to not reduce the budget for services for the poor by very much. "What is very much?" we asked. The answer needed to be specific in order for it to be actionable. After a bit of discussion, they agreed that they could absorb cuts of no more than 3 percent.

The leader and the team members work together to define the walls of this cube and ensure that everyone understands and accepts this "what" and "why." Then the leader stands back and lets the teams operate inside the cube. As a leader I don't care how they deliver the results in the desired timeframe and budget as long as they do so without crossing any of the walls of the cube. The teams own the inside of the cube. That is their "how." They can navigate and make the time/cost/task/resource trade-offs they need in order to deliver the results without crossing the walls of the cube. As a leader, I monitor only the walls of the cube. I never monitor what the team is doing inside the cube.

For example, my storage administrator Sam told me that unless we did something to expand our data storage, we would be out of room in about six months. Had I been a micromanager, and ignored my lack of deep knowledge of data storage technologies, I would have told Sam to buy more storage sometime before we ran out of space. Instead, I worked through the Macro-Cube of this project with him. We established the expected results: We wanted to double our storage capacity in fewer than four months for less than $X and without violating our storage standard. Those were the walls of his cube in completing this project. Sam owned all of the project "hows." He met with various vendors and checked with his peers. He sometimes asked for my opinion, but I kept my answers to opinions—I did not want to take away any of his ownership or stifle his innovation by telling him how to do anything. When I asked for a project report, I asked him only about the status of the walls. Would he be done within four months, would we at least double our capacity, would we spend no more than $X, and would we maintain a homogeneous storage environment? If the answers were all "Yes," life was good.

Sam discovered that about 75 percent of our current storage was duplicated files. For example, someone sends a document to 20 people for review and 18 of the 20 retain the document. Such activity resulted in 19 duplicate files. If all we did was de-duplicate such storage, we would more than double our capacity. His analysis also showed that a pretty decent percentage of our storage was allocated to rarely accessed data. Sam explored some ideas. What if we pushed that off to some type of archived storage? This archival storage could be slow compared to the more active storage while freeing up space. So he negotiated with our current storage provider and explained our desire to stay with them—but only if they helped us with some pricing concessions. With this done, he came to me with his proposal for expanding our storage. Through a combination of data de-duplication, archived storage, and price concessions, we could just about quadruple our storage capacity, improve service levels, slow down our rate of storage growth, spend about half of the budget, and do so well ahead of the schedule. Stated differently, Sam's ownership and motivation generated a much better result than what I would have done.

This experience and countless others have taught us that we need to be careful about where we focus our leadership attention. The focus should be on "what" and "why" and never "how." That does not mean we never do any "how" work. But our "how" work is tied to our leadership role. The "what" and "why" of our role are things like succession planning for the organization. We own "how" we deliver a successful succession plan. Our "what" and "why" include how our department will help the organization achieve its goals. Our "hows" then turn into the "what" and the "why" for our staff and teams. If we think of such cascading Macro-Cubes, alignment becomes more logical and visible.

This Macro-Cube concept also applies to processes and methods. Too often we implement processes that constrain innovation and destroy motivation. What if, from a leadership perspective, we focused the definition of process and methodology on the "what" and "why" of the process? One "what" in my software development process is that we achieve the shortest possible time between development and testing. Why? To reduce the time and resources it takes to eliminate bugs. The less time it takes to find and fix a bug, the lower the costs, the happier the customer, and the more resource capacity I create. But, I leave the "how" of this "what" to my teams. Should they co-locate testing personnel with my development engineers? That is up to them. Should they implement automating testing so that software engineers can know at least daily what bugs they created?

They own that decision. Should the testing engineers write user stories to simplify the creation of the test cases? Whatever it takes to achieve the "what." As long as the process satisfies the goals of this particular cube without breaking through any of the walls, I will be happy.

In this case, the Macro-Cube also includes a wall for process simplicity (the "what" for any process should include that it be simple, easy to follow, and not bureaucratic). Too often, we human beings, left to ourselves, will define and implement processes that are overly complex. And remember, complexity is the enemy of agility and innovation.

This Macro-Cube image can be a very effective tool for making sure that you, as a leader, do not encroach where you do not belong. It can also be effective in leading up with your own micromanaging manager, should you ever find yourself working for one. I once accepted a challenging assignment from the CEO of the company. Because of the dependencies and critical nature of this project, the CEO started to check in on my work with increasingly irritating frequency. My normally hands-off boss became, in just a few days, a micromanager. My frustration with him grew and his frustration with my frustration grew. One day, after he asked me to immediately make some very minor changes to how I tracked the project dependencies, I walked into his office with a blank piece of paper. I asked for just a few minutes of his time. I then drew the outline of a Macro-Cube for the project.

"Jon," I said, "If I understand my assignment correctly, I need to deliver these results." I then labeled the walls of the project cube. Jon wondered what I was up to but agreed with my assessment of the "what" for the project. I continued, "You chose me for this project because you think I have the ability to get this done. But you are treating me as if I am not capable of delivering this assignment."

Jon looked shocked. "Not at all. You have my full confidence."

I then referred to the drawing of the Macro-Cube and said, "You are asking, on a fairly regular basis, how I am going to deliver the results. In effect, you are climbing inside the walls of this cube with me and tracing my steps as I work to deliver the results. Normally, I would not mind that, but your tracking how I get this done is getting in the way. I spend so much time giving you updates that it is slowing my progress."

"But I do need to know what is going on—this is a critical project!" he said.

I referred again to the drawing. "It seems that your focus should be on whether or not I deliver the expected results—the walls in this drawing—and not how I get that done. Right now, you seem more focused on how I am doing things than on whether or not I will deliver the right things."

Jon paused for a moment and finally said, "I get it now. I should be asking you about the project deliverables and not the mechanics of your project management. Is that right?"

"That is it in a nutshell. Thank you."

After that, when Jon asked me a question, he asked whether or not he was "inside my cube." If I told him "Yes," he backed off. If I answered "No," I did a quick update on the status of the expected results (but never on how I was getting things done).

This visual is not perfect, but it can help both leaders and teams develop a feeling of ownership. At a minimum, this model asks us to define the expected results and other requirements, including timelines, available resources, standards to follow, purpose, and other considerations like uncertainty and complexity. With these defined, both leaders and teams know what they own—and don't own.

Ownership is critical in changing and improving culture. It is hard to own something that is not well-defined. This model encourages that definition.

In Summary

Because we sometimes have a tendency to tell our team how to do things, we need to constantly remind ourselves to get out of the "how" business and stay in the "what" and "why" business. Once we have done that, we need to make sure that we do not take that ownership away; otherwise, we stand between our teams and their ownership and development. In this chapter, we have provided some tools for you to help your teams take ownership, for you to not take it back, and to work with your teams to define their ownership (the walls of the Macro-Cube).

Then, stand back and let them deliver.

References

[1] Buckingham, Marcus, and Coffman, Curt. *First, Break All the Rules: What the Worlds' Greatest Managers Do Differently*. New York: Simon & Schuster, 1999, page 117.

CHAPTER 6

BUSINESS ALIGNMENT TOOLS

The Big Ideas

- To get to Energy and Innovation we must align team ownership to what creates a unique value proposition, in line with the goals of the business.
- The team must be clear on the product's purpose. Is it aligned with the goals of the business?
- Get everyone—stakeholders, delivery teams, and business interests—to understand and agree to what generates value for their customers.

Are We Aligned with the Company's Business Goals?

For a quite a long time now, when research organizations survey to find the top issues and opportunities for IT leaders, misalignment of team goals with the organization is one of the top responses. For quite a long time now, when research organizations survey to find what company presidents believe is the most pressing issue with their IT leaders, alignment with the organization is one of the top responses. It seems alignment just might be a pretty big deal.

Why does alignment matter? Because a critical component of ownership is knowing what to own. Think of the power that comes from an entire organization of people working together, in concert, to achieve the organization's goals. These are people who understand the unique, compelling value proposition of the organization and who can directly link everything they do to the organization's goals and value proposition.

When we understand how we align, we make better decisions about which products to develop, which processes to improve, and which features and functions to include. Our focus changes from getting things done to getting the right things done. Without alignment, ownership suffers.

In this chapter, we present three tools you can use to improve alignment. All three work together to cover most of your alignment needs. As you read about these tools, think about how you can apply them to your current projects. Think about how you can use them to help your teams take ownership.

Purpose-Based Alignment Model

In this book, we have talked about the importance of increasing ownership. Ideally, we align our team's ownership with the purpose and goals of the organization. But how can we, and they, know what those are?

Our Purpose-Based Alignment Model, detailed in our first book, *Stand Back and Deliver* [1], is a simple (but sometimes not an easy) way for us to define the design goals of our projects, products, processes, and organizations. The tool provides a vocabulary and model that teams can use to build a common, aligned understanding of the business goals.

The model is shown in Figure 6.1.

Using Purpose-Based Alignment, we jointly look at our processes, business rules, plans, et cetera in two dimensions: Market Differentiation and Mission Critical. Because Purpose-Based Alignment is a very useful way to align to organizational goals, let's take a few moments to describe the resulting categories.

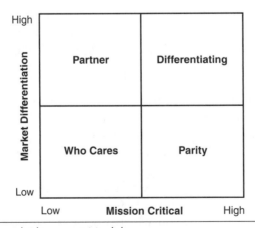

FIGURE 6.1   Purpose-Based Alignment Model

The processes or plans that are both Market Differentiating and Mission Critical are those things that create our competitive advantage and link directly to our strategy. These are the things we must do better than anyone else if we want to win new customers and gain market share. This is what defines our unique value proposition. To ensure the proper degree of focus on the differentiating things, we should limit how many of our activities fall into this category. It is important that we focus on market leadership for only these few things. To be aligned, we focus our innovation and creativity on these products and processes.

The vast majority of our work is Mission Critical and *not* Market Differentiating. However, we must have it to go to market. The purpose of such activities is to be at parity with the marketplace and customer expectations—to hold our current market share. For example, unless we are in the payroll business, most of us do not create competitive advantage because of our payroll processing excellence. Thus, we should not spend time or resources thinking about how to make our payroll processing better than it has to be. But we cannot be payroll processing laggards. If we cannot pay our employees correctly or on time, they just might decide to take their skills elsewhere. In practice, we want to implement simple, best-practices-based business rules for these parity activities. It is common to misalign to the parity processes, practices, and products. Too often, organizations and teams overinvest in parity. But we also cannot underinvest in parity.

And the gaps could be areas where we are currently better than best practices. Remember, when it comes to parity, we do not want to overinvest or overcomplicate. We should also avoid any parity risks. Because of the mission-critical nature of these parity activities, we don't want to be taking any chances. Finally, we can generate potentially incredible amounts of capacity from our parity products, systems, and processes as we have typically overinvested in them over the years.

To optimize the business value of parity activities, we use the following parity rules:

- Standardize—minimize exception handling.
- Simplify—complex parity processes rob us of both resources and agility.
- Adopt best practices—we don't need to invent parity; we just need to learn it.

It might be possible for us to create competitive advantage without having to develop mission-critical capabilities. For such things, we seek and engage partners. For example, we once worked with a publisher that created competitive advantage with its unique content and partnered with a technology company to extend this content advantage by creating its market's first digital capabilities—capabilities the publisher had no desire to create on its own. But such partnerships to create competitive advantage are rare.

Finally, there might be some things that are neither Market Differentiating nor Mission Critical. We should minimize the time and resources spent on these "Who cares?" activities.

Four Questions

Purpose-Based Alignment is a powerful alignment tool if we can correctly define what is differentiating for us. To get that answer, we use the Four Questions. These are

- Who do we serve? This defines our target markets and market segments.
- What do they need and want most? For each segment we determine what matters to them.
- What do we do—better than anyone else—to meet those needs and wants? This is where we align our organization to market needs. This is where we specifically define how we create competitive advantage.
- What is the best way for us to deliver our products and services? Sometimes it is our delivery model that creates our competitive advantage.

Accurate alignment increases the likelihood that we will not underinvest in what creates competitive advantage while also not overinvesting in parity activities. The net result is accelerated growth at lower costs and risks.

Anyone can use the Four Questions to identify what creates sustainable competitive advantage. If the senior leadership has done this, the team can align to that. But the local leadership and teams can ask and answer the Four Questions themselves in order to understand and align to the organization's unique value proposition. With the differentiating defined, our next step is to turn this into decision filters that we can use for all current and future decisions. These decision filters are invaluable. We can share them throughout our team and the organization to ensure that everyone has a common understanding of our priorities. For every product, process, project, feature, or function, we can use our decision filters to ensure that we align the product, process, project, feature, or function to how we create competitive advantage.

If differentiating for us is our "one-stop-shop" product platform, our decision filter might be

Will [this] help us innovate our product platform?

If we are pondering an enhancement to our internal benefits program, we can ask, "Will enhancements to our benefits program help us innovate our product platform?" No. This does not mean that the benefits enhancements are not a priority. This means that we will follow the parity rules and simplify, standardize, and base on best practices our benefits enhancements. There is no need to waste our innovation on our benefits program.

If we create competitive advantage because we have the best market data in the world, our decision filter might be

Will [this] help us gather better data?

If our product backlog includes a project to develop predictive data modeling, we might want to do something truly innovative as we design our predictive modeling tool.

This purpose alignment thing sounds easy but it can sometimes be a challenge. There is a natural desire in all of us to think that what we do is differentiating and deserves innovation. After all, how do we think we ended up with so much complexity in our parity processes? One of the ways to test our decisions about how we create competitive advantage is to use the Billboard Test.

The Billboard Test

If something really is differentiating, we should focus our sales, marketing, and advertising on this product, service, or capability. In other words, would we ever post what we think is differentiating on a billboard?

Looking at the decision filter examples in the previous section, would we ever purchase a billboard to tell the world about our employee benefits program? Hopefully not.

But would we invest in a billboard that describes how we use predictive modeling to improve the quality of our data? You bet we would.

Note that purpose alignment does not define the priority of a product, project, process, feature, or function—just whether or not it deserves innovation. To determine priority we use the Business Value Model (which we describe in the next section).

Using the Purpose-Based Alignment Model with your team, define the differentiators for your project/product and what the parity is. Does it align with the business goals of the organization? Do the differentiators align? Do the parity activities align with business parity?

Along with the decision filters, having a well-known billboard is a powerful way of sharing the vision, which enables our teams to take aligned ownership.

At the risk of either boring you or being completely redundant in our explanation of how to use the Purpose-Based Alignment Model to achieve organization and project alignment, we offer a final example.

Not too long ago, I was asked by the CEO of a medical device company to help that company select a new enterprise resource planning (ERP) system. The company needed to upgrade its systems to improve its margins and throughput. But how could it do this in a market-aligned way?

At that time, the company had gathered the requirements for the new system and compiled these into a very nice software selection spreadsheet. The spreadsheet contained just over 300 rows. Each row described a needed piece of functionality. The spreadsheet also had columns for the functionality, a weighted score for the functionality (between 0.1 and 0.9 depending on the criticality of the functionality), and a score for each of the major software vendors. This score would measure the excellence of that vendor's handling of the required functionality. A piece of the spreadsheet looked like what is shown in Figure 6.2.

Funtionality	Weight	Vendor A	Vendor B	Vendor C
Inventory Costing	0.8			
Lot Tracking	0.9			
Time Keeping	0.3			

FIGURE 6.2   Example of the Software Selection Scoring Spreadsheet

During the software selection, the company would send a request for information to each of the vendors and then, using the vendors' responses, fill in the vendor scores and make their decision.

With the permission of the CEO, I asked for time with the management team. We met in one of their conference rooms. I explained purpose alignment as I drew it on the whiteboard.

"How do you create competitive advantage? What specifically do you do better than anyone else?" I asked.

I then asked each of the Four Questions, and we dove into the discussion of how this company won in the marketplace. There was a range of answers, but we quickly centered on the design of their products. They made products that were engineered for ease of use. Their products were much simpler for surgeons to use. The focus of their engineering teams was to find ways to shorten the time it took for surgeons to complete a surgery.

With this in mind, we agreed to the company's decision filter: Will [this] enable surgeons to simplify and shorten surgeries? If so, the company would innovate. If not, it was a parity activity, decision, process, et cetera.

The company could now use this decision filter to align any and all decisions to how the company created its unique value in the marketplace. The next step was to use this decision filter to align the ERP selection and implementation project.

Recall that the company needed to improve its margins and throughput and felt that this project was critical in achieving those goals. But what is the best way to achieve those goals? By aligning the project around how the company created competitive advantage.

Would any of the more than 300 desired pieces of functionality allow surgeons to simplify and shorten surgeries? Would, for example, superior inventory costing simplify and shorten surgeries? No way. Would better lot tracking? Not likely.

In other words, their software selection was a parity decision and as such, should follow the parity rules of

- Standardize
- Simplify
- Adopt best practices

In looking at the desired functionality, we could not see a single item that would simplify and shorten surgeries. And because each of the three vendors' products supported industry best practices for all of the functionality, we decided to take functionality completely out of the decision. It did not matter who did lot tracking better. All that mattered was that lot tracking was present. Did one of the vendors do inventory costing better? That did not matter because parity is the world of doing things as well as others and "better than" might create complexity.

To select the software, we brainstormed and prioritized considerations (which we describe in the Business Value Model in the next section). The number one consideration was time to benefit followed by licensing and implementation costs. We used these to select the vendor that could come into the project with an existing configuration designed for a medical device company. And because we had agreed that all of the functionality was in the parity category, we also agreed that there would not be any customizations to the software. This approach resulted in a very successful, lower-cost, faster project. This was all because the company recognized the difference between differentiating and parity.

Business Value Model

We want our teams, when they take ownership, to make decisions that align to our business value. But, before they can, we and they need to know the answer to the following question: What is value and how can we define it?

Let me answer this question with a very succinct answer:

> We create value when we focus our innovation on what creates our competitive advantage, and then we do almost everything else just well enough.

Stated slightly differently, work does not create value if it does not directly support our competitive advantage. Likewise, we do not create value if we do everything else better than it has to be or if we do it poorly.

This is simple in theory but difficult in practice. Our natural tendency is to attempt to do all important activities in an exceptional way—even if doing so reduces the value we deliver. To help us make decisions that align to our business value, we have developed the Business Value Model (BVM). The BVM is designed to guide every decision we make about what creates value. We can use the model to help teams understand the business priorities. Working with our teams to build a well-understood, common view of the business value priorities of our options provides a powerful guide to our teams, enabling them to take ownership that is well aligned with the organization's goals.

This section provides an overview of the BVM. If you would like a more detailed explanation, please see our previous book, *Stand Back and Deliver* [1].

The BVM consists of three drivers of value: (1) Purpose, (2) Costs and Benefits, and (3) Considerations, as shown in Figure 6.3.

Purpose

In the previous section, we introduced and showed some examples of purpose alignment. In the context of the BVM, the important distinction is that line between the differentiating and the parity activities. We generate value when we do the differentiating things better than anyone else. We generate value when we do the parity things in a parity way (simplified, streamlined, standardized, and based on best practices).

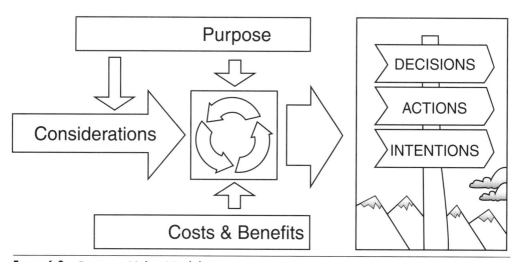

FIGURE 6.3 Business Value Model

Costs and Benefits

We are all familiar with traditional cost/benefit analysis. However, cost/benefit analysis only works when we can, with some precision, quantify the costs and the benefits. Because cost/benefit analysis is typically some type of calculation, this calculation fails if we lack cost/benefit precision—and in a world with an uncertain future and where ambiguity is the only certainty, this calculation fails the vast majority of the time. In our experience, while we might be able to reasonably estimate costs, the benefit side of the calculation often comes down to an educated guess—or worse, a really bad guess. Or even worse, a number that we know in advance will meet the investment criteria! If the uncertainty in cost is ±25 percent and the uncertainty in benefit is ±50 percent (both fairly reasonable estimates), then the uncertainty in the cost/benefit ratio is close to ±85 percent! Essentially, a random number! In other words, be careful with how you use cost/benefit calculations in your decision making. If you do not have and cannot acquire reasonably precise numbers, your calculations will be of little value. And if you are depending on uncertain calculations to make your decisions, your decisions might also be of little value. The BVM anticipates these problems with cost/benefit calculations by including considerations. If your uncertainty is on this order, then you will have to make an appropriate judgment call to decide which figures to use while recognizing the significant uncertainty in the estimate.

Considerations

We don't want to ignore costs, benefits, or any other driver of value just because we cannot quantify it, and so the BVM includes Considerations. Considerations are the drivers or inhibitors of value that we cannot quantify. Depending on the process, project, or activity, Considerations might include

- Time to benefit
- Market window
- Alignment to goals
- Compliance
- Market uncertainty
- Technical uncertainty
- Technical complexity
- Market complexity
- Internal capability
- Partner capability

And a whole host of others.

When we define value, we use the BVM as follows:

- Be clear on what is the organization's sustainable competitive advantage. This is what defines our differentiating activities. We then map our projects, processes, products, features, functions, et cetera to differentiating versus parity and establish the design goal. Is this something we should do better than anyone else or as well as everyone else?
- With some precision, estimate the quantifiable costs and benefits.
- Brainstorm and prioritize the Considerations for our projects, processes, products, features, functions, et cetera.

This combination of Purpose, Costs and Benefits, and Considerations defines the BVM for our specific projects, processes, products, features, functions, et cetera. This is not a number but a market- and strategy-aligned decision framework we can use to make a whole host of decisions. With this model we can determine which actions will generate the highest value. If we do the highest-value things first, we achieve Value-First.

Perhaps an example will help.

We were working with a product team that developed software for the healthcare industry. This company was growing rapidly and building toward a hoped-for initial public offering. The team had a nearly endless backlog of requests and needed to know how to prioritize the backlog. Answer: Value-First. But what defined value for this team?

As a first step, we answered the Four Questions:

1. Who do we serve?
2. What do they want and need most?
3. What do we do—better than anyone else—to meet those needs and wants?
4. What is the best way for us to deliver our products and services?

This company differentiated themselves in the market by offering an integrated portfolio of healthcare software products. The company's competitors each had point solutions that were better than any of the individual products in the company's integrated portfolio, but no one could touch them when it came to product integration. From the perspective of purpose alignment, this company needed to constantly innovate in integration and quickly add new, parity products to their portfolio. This meant that everything else the company and team did was parity. At the company level, the parity activities included their internal IT operations, their customer service, their accounting, et cetera. At the product level, the parity activities included the functionality of the individual products in the portfolio (they could approximately mimic the features developed by others). With these design goals established, we next looked at their product backlog.

Their backlog included both differentiating and parity projects. We quickly sorted through the planned functionality of these projects and identified some opportunities for a change in design and focus.

One of the projects in their backlog was a customer-requested product that seemed particularly challenging. This product anticipated using several bleeding-edge technologies to deliver new capabilities for this large and very demanding customer. From the perspective of purpose alignment, this product did not fit. The company did not develop or deliver any bleeding-edge point solutions. Yet, there were other considerations—they wanted to satisfy this customer.

Another project delivered integrations that directly supported their ease-of-use goals. But the bulk of the portfolio consisted of projects that clearly fit in the parity category. For these, the design goal was clear but how should they be prioritized?

We started with the customer-requested product. In terms of business value this project would be a one-off that consumed quite a bit of resources with little direct benefit—except for keeping this large and important customer happy. Logic required that they drop this project. Emotion (and the vice president of sales) demanded they do the project. Before taking this decision any further, we agreed to first brainstorm and prioritize the considerations we would use to rationalize and prioritize the portfolio. After a bit of discussion, we listed, in order:

- Aligns to long- and short-term goals. The most important short-term goal being to increase margins in anticipation of our initial public offering.
- Improves our customer satisfaction scores.
- Improves our ease-of-use competitive advantage.

Based on these, the priorities became easier. The highest priority was to complete the several parity projects that improved margins. The customer-requested project would improve the customer satisfaction score—but for just one customer—and so was given a low priority. The vice president of sales agreed to work with that customer to reduce some of their most challenging requirements because those were what created the need for the bleeding-edge technologies. Finally, the project to improve ease of use was given the lowest priority. How can this be? After all, shouldn't a project that improves competitive advantage always have the highest priority? Not if we remember that both differentiating and parity are equally important. At that point, the company's focus was on getting ready for an initial public offering, and boosting margins was the highest priority, a business goal. That might change in the future and so the team agreed to review and revise their considerations on a regular basis.

You might have noticed that nowhere in this discussion did the team include known costs or benefits. That's because they could not precisely determine either of those for any of these projects. Remember, we include—and possibly rely on—considerations to help us analyze costs and benefits that we cannot precisely know.

How about one more example to show how the BVM quickly yields quality decisions? Our company was spending nearly $1 million a year on conference-calling services. As we grew, this amount would only get bigger. I called the team together to talk about what we could do to reduce these costs—while not making anything else worse!

The team used the BVM to create a framework for their ownership of the project. They started with Purpose. Conference calling is a parity service. It is mission critical, but no one does business with us because we are the market leaders in holding conference calls. Thus, we would acquire rather than invent conference-calling technology. Also, we would not make any customizations to that technology but use it "out of the box." Its mission-critical nature meant that we could not be lousy at providing conference-calling services. Given our need to reduce risk for a mission-critical service, the team limited its choices to market-leading, proven options. On the Considerations side of the BVM, the team considered that one of our goals was to move as many of our IT services to the cloud as possible. This along with considering only market-leading, proven options were our high-priority considerations. With these defined, the team brainstormed the options and mapped them to the BVM they had developed.

From a known cost/benefit view, the best choice was to acquire and bring in-house our own conference bridge technology. For a total cost of around $250,000 we would never again pay for any conference calling. To spend $250,000 to save $1,000,000 (and growing) a year made perfect sense. However, this violated the consideration to move more and more services to the cloud. The team balanced the known costs/benefits with the "cloud" consideration and decided that it still made the most sense to pursue the internal conference bridge. The members had balanced the options against the goals. Best of all, the team owned the results and they ensured that the project was a success. Their ownership included not only the successful installation of the conference bridge but also moving every audio conference user (over 2,000 of them) seamlessly onto the new system.

Value is sometimes hard to define and even harder to deliver. We must remember two things:

- It is the customer that defines value.
- We create value when we focus our innovation on what creates our competitive advantage, and then we do almost everything else just well enough.

This will help our teams make sound decisions that define and prioritize their actions. They have ownership.

Product/Project Inception Planning

The first time I held a product inception session was to prepare for the second release of a major product. As a starting point, the team presented the screen shots of the previous version of the product and the work they had done to prepare for the second release. As the team reviewed the work, people started asking some hard questions.

"Where did that come from?" Paul asked as he pointed to one of the pages.

There was silence in the room. A major change had been added by the business without collaborating with the development team. This had happened many times and was a major point of conflict between the two groups. According to the development team, these unplanned efforts caused more disruption than value.

How could something sneak into the product without someone noticing and asking why? Or without someone wondering how it happened, because the new feature did not align with any of the goals for the looming product release?

Over the years, we have developed and refined a process that provides tools that align product planning around customer value and that get everyone to agree as to the product customers, the product purpose, and the role each team will play to launch a successful product. This process consists of the following steps:

1. Assemble a cross-functional team with representatives from every major product development and support function.
2. Present and agree as to "why this product?"
3. Build a map of the customer journey, end-to-end.
4. Create a prioritized list of all the things the product could do to touch and improve the customer journey.
5. Write these as stories from the point of view of the customer. These stories include the value the customer should get from the product.
6. Create a billboard for this product—this is the core message and value proposition of the product.
7. Write decision filters for the product—you will use these to filter every and all decisions about product features and priorities.
8. Build high-level wireframes or storyboards—a low-fidelity picture of the product.
9. Identify the features that deliver the minimum viable product.
10. Write and prioritize user stories for the next release.
11. Discuss the required tasks and roles and ask the team which product development elements they will own.
12. Agree on the process for making decisions and how decisions will be communicated—both to the team and to the stakeholders.
13. If there were any issues that could not be resolved in the session, list them as action items and let team members volunteer to define and deliver a plan that resolves the issues.
14. Ask someone to volunteer to write up and distribute all the outputs.
15. Agree as to how the team will hold each other accountable.

Where Do We Start?

The product inception session is a day-and-a-half to two-day process. It involves anyone with an interest in what is going to be built, those who will build it, and those who will support it. This means not just the product manager and the lead developers but customer support, marketing, sales, user experience designers, or anyone whose work will be touched by the creation of this product. In putting an inception session together, we tell everyone that we will be making concrete decisions about the direction and functionality of the product. We remind them that if they choose to delegate these important decisions to someone else, they had better delegate to someone they trust to make these decisions. Otherwise, they should plan on attending with us—after all, what is more important than defining the products that will define the company's future?

This can be a very intense meeting. The goal of the session is to make lasting decisions about product markets, purpose, direction, and high-level plans. With the goal of finalizing some of these critical, up-front decisions, those who can and should make lasting decisions should attend. This session requires a high level of focus—people participating should plan on being disconnected from their normal lives. They should put away their cell phones and laptops and tell everyone in their lives that they will respond to e-mail later. What you don't want is to have the group make a decision while someone is texting and have that person say, "When did we decide that? I don't agree because . . . ." If this happens, it likely creates churn, and churn not only wastes time, it frustrates the participants. In many cases, this product vision development is one of the most important activities in the organization—you can afford to be off the grid in order to get this right.

One other way to reduce churn is to observe a rule such as if the product manager leaves the room, the discussion stops and everyone waits for the product manager to return.

The goal of this process is to reduce the churn and the handoffs and potential miscommunication of product development and launch. You need to understand what you are creating and why.

The process beings with . . .

Why Are We Building This Product?

The planning begins with the business presenting the answers to the following questions from Marty Cagan's book, *Inspired: How to Create Products Customers Love* [2]:

1. Exactly what problem will this solve? (value proposition)
2. For whom are we solving this problem? (target market)
3. How big is the opportunity? (market size)
4. How will we measure success? (metrics/revenue strategy)
5. What alternatives are out there now? (competitive landscape)
6. Why are we best suited to pursue this? (our differentiator)
7. Why now? (market window)
8. How will we get this product to market? (go-to-market strategy)
9. What factors are critical to success? (solution requirements)
10. Given the above, what's the recommendation? (go or no go)

Customer Experience Journey

The train system in America, Amtrak, wanted to grow their market and attract more people to train transportation. One thought was to redesign and modernize their train cars. However, the actual train ride was only a portion of the broad customer experience. So they took a closer look at the customer experience. This involved the desire to take a trip, finding Amtrak, entering the train station, buying a ticket, waiting, boarding, riding, arriving, and continuing.

This journey looks like the diagram presented in Figure 6.4, using data from Peer Insight, LLC.

When you consider this entire customer experience journey, you factor in things like entering Grand Central Station in New York City—now that is a great customer experience. It makes a train station a destination.

By mapping the entire experience, we think about how potential customers learn about where the train goes, how frequently, and for how much. How should we do that? A website or travel application? Alliances? What advice can we give them to help in the planning? How do we

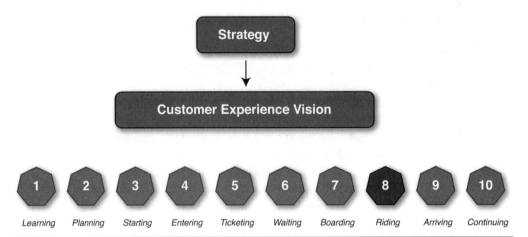

FIGURE 6.4   Amtrak customer experience journey

personalize the experience and the planning? What can we do to identify and profile different market segments? How can we streamline the entire process—streamline ticketing, reduce waiting, and improve boarding? What about the actual train ride? What would make dining better? Should there be sightseeing along the way? When you consider the entire experience and how you can touch and influence the experience, it opens up both thinking and the possibilities. As a result of this customer experience journey mapping, Amtrak started to focus on and include a broader range of services for its customers. Amtrak identified where its customer experience gaps existed and how they could fill the gaps. As another example, airlines have certainly taken advantage of the continuing part by asking after you have purchased a ticket if you need a rental car or hotel and how they can help you with that.

In general, the customer experience journey contains the following phases:

- Discover needs: Your customer has a need and discovers your product.
- Consider the options: Compare with competitors, read reviews.
- Engagement: Try before they buy.
- Evaluation: Make the buy decision.
- Purchase: Set up an account and pay.
- Delivery/installation.
- Usage: Support, customer service, billing, upgrades.

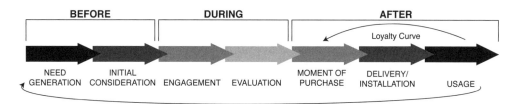

FIGURE 6.5   Customer experience journey

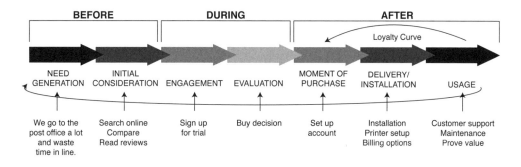

FIGURE 6.6   Customer experience journey example

It looks like the process illustrated in Figure 6.5.

Let's look at an example. How would you develop a product for buying postage stamps online? The customer experience journey would look like Figure 6.6.

Now, where does your product touch the customer experience and journey? What do you have to build to ensure a full customer experience? What are the touch points for the online stamps example?

You would need a website, a free trial period, an account setup, a way to accept a credit card, help with setting up a printer, billing options, customer support, and diagnostics. And, you need an easy-to-use interface.

Create your customer experience journey using the labels in Figure 6.6, and ask the attendees, in small groups, to address the customer journey. Have the team use sticky notes, one answer on each sticky note, to give as many answers as they want. For example, for initial consideration you provide a website, ads in print media, TV ads, social media, e-mails, ads on invoices to current customers, and so on. Put the labels on large pages and have each team add their sticky notes. Then, mark which ones you need to build—these are your touch points.

And just to make sure you did not miss anything, validate your map of the journey with several of your customers.

What Will Delight Your Customer?

What does your customer want to be able to do with your product? You need to create a prioritized list of all the things your customer wants the product to do.

Again, using sticky notes and fat pens, write all the things you feel your customers want and would find of value. If you have customers attending the session, you get bonus points because you can get real data in real time! Group the answers and prioritize them based on value to customers.

Write these from the point of view of the customer, including the business value. The stories usually take the form:

> As a <type of customer>, I want to <action> so that <business value>.

Make sure no solution is in the action and don't forget the business value. These should be at a high level and are often referred to as epics.

Which epics will differentiate your product from your competitors' products? And which epics are what customers must have but all your competitors have in their products? The differentiators help you gain market share. The others are parity and will hold your current market share. Both are mission critical and must be done to go to market. For more on this, see the Purpose-Based Alignment Model at the beginning of this chapter.

Let's look at our example of online postage. An epic would be something like the following:

> As a stamp purchaser, I want to buy stamps online so that I can save time by not going to the post office and waiting in line.

Stay Focused

Let's say you buy a billboard to advertise your product. (The Billboard Test is described in detail earlier in this chapter.) What would you put on it? Remember, it must be short because someone has limited time to read it. It could start: "Buy our product because . . . ." A famous billboard from Southwest, a low-cost airline in America, reads: "The low-cost airline." For our online postage product, it might read, "Stamps without the wait!" or "Stamps: what you want, any time."

Think of the billboard that describes your product. Write your product's concise, compelling value proposition. This decision filter helps you stay focused on the what and why of your product.

Now let's convert the billboard to a decision filter. Every story, every task must pass the decision filter. With this tool, we will filter out all the tasks that might be way cool but are not needed for this product and will not directly create meaningful value. You can now cascade this decision filter through the entire organization so that everyone knows how your company and your products and services create competitive advantage.

Returning to the example of Southwest Airlines, we can imagine a decision filter such as "Will this help us be *the* low-cost airline?"

When other airlines start charging passengers for checked baggage, Southwest Airlines could ask, "Will charging for checked baggage help us be the low-cost airline?" Absolutely not. Southwest Airlines decided to find other ways to increase profits but not at the cost of not being the low-cost airline.

When people asked the flight attendants if they could have chicken Caesar salad on the plane, the attendants could ask themselves, "Does that help us be the low-cost airline?" The most expensive thing in the airline business is time on the ground. Putting the salads on board would increase the time on the ground. The attendants could make the decision themselves and explain it to the people making the request.

For online postage, the decision filters would be, "Does this reduce the waiting time for stamps?" and "Does this help customers get stamps when they want them?"

What to Build First

Now that we have an idea what the product will do for a customer, let's, at a high level, define what your customer sees and/or does. For products with lots of interfaces to the user, develop high-level wireframes using the process that follows. If there is minimal user interface or the wireframes are already done, then you could storyboard the customer's workflow. You may want to do both.

High-Level Wireframes

A wireframe is often called a screen blueprint. It is what the customer sees on the interface screen.

This part of the workshop is often called a design studio. We want to generate some of the screens for your product at the high level. We want to illuminate, sketch, present, critique, *and* iterate. You can read more about the process in Will Evans's articles [3, 4].

Basically, in small groups, pick a design challenge from one of the high-value epics and work in groups to iterate to develop a screen design. Because you might have five or six epics, let each group work on a different epic. We are looking for quantity not quality. During a critique you are only allowed to say "this solves the problem by . . ." and not say things like "I like it" or "I don't like it."

Divide the group into small teams. In the first round

- Have each individual within the group fold a single sheet of paper into eight sections and sketch up to eight different ideas with text and minimal annotation (10 minutes).
- Split each group in half and each individual pitches his ideas for 2 minutes followed by short critique—no longer than 3 minutes (20 minutes total).

In the second round you refine the work.

- Each individual uses one sheet of paper to refine one preferred concept by adding more details based on collective feedback (it's okay to use another's ideas) (10 minutes).
- Each individual presents his concept to the group (2 minutes followed by a 3-minute critique).

In the third round there is more refining.

- Each group collaborates on one prototype using one sheet (10 minutes).
- Each team presents their concept's prototype to the entire group (2 minutes) and gets a 3-minute critique.

Storyboarding

There are several kinds of storyboarding. One that was developed at the Walt Disney Studios in the early 1930s is a sequence of images of what your customer might do with your product.

Other people might find a workflow diagram helpful. However, it must be very high level and should not include a lot of detail. You are just looking to see if everyone has a clear understanding of the purpose of the product.

If you are upgrading an existing system, another way to get clarity is to map the movement of the new data through the current system, highlighting what needs to be added.

Minimum Viable Product

What is the minimum set of features to deploy to a subset of customers to get feedback and nothing more? That is the minimum viable product (MVP). Mark on your wireframes or your storyboard what the MVP is for your product. Next, write user stories from the customer's point of view in the same structure as the epics just for this MVP. Prioritize them by their business value using the Business Value Model (described earlier in this chapter).

Governance

How are you all going to work together? Talk about the roles in the team and what their responsibilities are. Who is your product manager, project leader, architect, resource manager?

New thoughts, ideas, and suggestions are going to come up. Some features on your list of things to do may not be built for one reason or another. Create a process for making these decisions and develop a communication plan to distribute those decisions

Accountability

Any issues that could not be resolved in the meeting need to be listed. These actions need volunteers to take each item and provide a due date. Don't forget to have a volunteer write up and distribute all the work on the walls.

Finally, ask the team how they will hold each other accountable. With that, the inception planning is done.

Meeting Logistics

Have plenty of the easel-size pads. I like to use the easel-size sticky notes and have blue tape in case they will not stick to the wall. Provide fat Sharpie pens in multiple colors, at least one pen for each attendee. You will need several pads of super sticky notes in multiple colors, at least one for every attendee. You will need some 3 × 5 notes and some slightly larger. You will need several sheets of 8½ × 11 paper for each attendee.

Make sure there are plenty of snacks and beverages. Inception planning can be a grueling, draining process.

Inception Planning Decision Filters

Use the following decision filters in your planning:

- Will this help us decide what will delight our customers?
- Will this help us understand what the product will do from a customer point of view?
- Will this help us to make decisions together?

In Summary

Purpose alignment, decision filters, and the Billboard Test are powerful tools for building ownership in our teams. These tools not only help teams understand where they should focus their innovation, but they also act as guidelines that improve the teams' decision making.

The starting point for aligned ownership is purpose alignment. Use this tool to quickly gain consensus on where to innovate and where good enough is good enough.

The natural outcome of purpose alignment is a set of decision filters you and your teams can use to align everything they do.

The inception planning process helps everyone understand why and what you are developing, but it also helps move the mindset to a customer viewpoint, what will delight the customer, and what will be valuable to the customer. It also makes clear that the business owns the problem and the delivery team owns the solution. They are not to cross over and take that ownership away, either way. And you can be clear that the purpose of this product aligns with the business goals of the organization.

By using these tools with our teams to explore our options, we help them fully understand the underlying reasons for what they are doing. In doing this we enable them to take ownership and make decisions in line with the overall business goals.

References

[1] Pixton, Pollyanna, Nickolaisen, Niel, Little, Todd, and McDonald, Kent. *Stand Back and Deliver: Accelerating Business Agility.* Boston: Addison-Wesley, 2010.

[2] Cagan, Marty. *Inspired: How to Create Products Customers Love.* Sunnyvale, CA: SVPG Press, 2008.

[3] Evans, Will. "Introduction to Design Studio Methodology." *UX Magazine,* August 24, 2011.

[4] ———. "The Design of a Design Studio." *UX Magazine,* September 29, 2011.

CHAPTER 7

DEALING HONESTLY WITH AMBIGUITY

The Big Ideas

- The worst time to make a commitment is when we know the least. We know the least at the beginning.
- We can iteratively accomplish two important tasks—proactively reduce risk and make meaningful commitments.
- One of the best-proven ways to honestly deal with ambiguity is to use iterative methods.

Easing the Need for Certainty

In Chapter 2, Trust and Ownership, we discussed the tension that exists between our desire for certainty and the fact that we live in an environment of increasing uncertainty. This tension exists, and it is highly unlikely that this tension will ever go away. As we hurtle toward an increasing pace of technology and rapid market change, uncertainty will increase, not shrink. At the same time, we continue to want to know what is going to happen so that we can plan and prepare for it.

Given this reality, what can we do? In this chapter, we present three tools you can use to partially satisfy the tension that comes from ambiguity.

Using Proactive Risk Management, we assess uncertainty as part of our risk analysis and make specific plans to decrease uncertainty. When risks, including uncertainty, are at a low enough level, we can make firm commitments. Until then, our commitments are as uncertain as the future.

We can make progress visible to improve access to status and information. It is easier to visually see progress, so display it this way and update it often.

Finally, using iterative methods is one of the best ways to deal with uncertainty, and so we give a short explanation of how and why to use such methods. This explanation is not comprehensive. There is much written about such methods and which ones to use and why. We hope to provide an overview of how such methods work because our book is filled with examples of how teams used iterative methods to achieve success.

Proactive Risk Management

In dealing honestly with ambiguity we need to recognize and deal with the pressure we and our teams are under to provide certainty. Proactive Risk Management is one tool that can satisfy the competing demands of certainty and ambiguity.

When is the absolutely, positively worst time to make a commitment? When we know the very least. So why do we keep doing it? Typically, we know the very least at the beginning of a project. Sure, we have done our planning and defined the contingencies, but at the beginning there is no way we can adequately anticipate the multiple uncertainties and complexities we will encounter. Yet this is when we make commitments for deliverables, costs, and timing. In other words, we set ourselves up to be wrong about deliverables, costs, and timing.

Some years ago, the National Aeronautic and Space Agency (NASA) conducted a comprehensive review of its ability to accurately predict the time, effort, and costs of its major software projects. NASA discovered that only 5 percent of the original project estimates came true. To think of this another way, if you make a commitment as to time, costs, resources, and scope, you will be wrong 95 percent of the time!

Why do we do this? There are at least two reasons. First, leaders seem to think if they have a date, they can control the outcomes. This, however, is delusional thinking, but they do it anyway. Second, the rest of our world wants to plan their lives around a date when we say we will be done. While our project might have dependencies to manage, the rest of the organization is dependent on us to meet our commitments. The pressure to make commitments when we know the least comes from many places.

Sometimes we, as leaders, apply this pressure. Sometimes the pressure comes from above and we cascade this pressure to our teams. All of this combines to create the commitment tension. Even though the very worst time to make a commitment is at the beginning (when we know the least), the rest of the organization wants us to commit (and keep our commitment) as early as possible. Marketing needs to develop product launch plans. Customer support needs to train their personnel. Internal departments need to plan for financial close activities, training, and process ripple effects. Thus begins the tension-filled dance. Everyone else presses us to make a commitment while we hedge as much and as long as possible. And how do we respond to the pressure to commit? By adding buffers to project tasks. If we double the estimated time to deliver the project, will that give us enough headroom to meet our commitment? Or would it be better to triple our estimates? If triple is enough, would quadruple be optimal? If meeting our early commitment is paramount, we do what we can to set ourselves up for success—even if that requires us to do planning and estimating contortions, and frustrates the rest of the business.

What if there was a better way? Admittedly, this way only works in a culture that is willing to accept a bit of ambiguity. But if we are honest with ourselves, it is not as if our current, commit-when-we-know-the-least method is working all that well. So, why not try something that might work? Perhaps we can do without the following scenario.

The team was required to make a "go-live" commitment during the initial planning phase. This was the date we would, for sure, be ready to turn on the new system. But, there were two questions we could not answer during planning. The first was uncertainty about the market. The new product was new and different enough that history could not inform us as to which features would have the largest impact. The second was a potentially complex technology. This new product required the development of technology that was new to the engineering team. The team members felt they had a reasonably good idea about how to build this technology but could not, with confidence, make a solid commitment. But, with the rest of the organization so dependent on the result of this project, the team was compelled to name the date their project would end and the new product would be released.

The project leader hedged by tripling the estimated time to develop the new, potentially complex technology. She also hedged by pushing the tasks associated with market uncertainty to the marketing team. Would the marketing team be able to resolve the market uncertainty? It was hard to know but at least it was no longer the project team's problem. With this done, the team made a commitment—fourteen months from then, the product would be ready! The sales department pushed back. Sales was anticipating the new product to reach its fourth quarter sales goals. That would only happen if the team completed the project in eight months; fourteen months was six months too late. The chief financial officer then weighed in. If Sales did not deliver on its sales goals, the company would not deliver the expected revenue and earnings goals. No, the team had to deliver in eight months!

The project sponsor gathered the team together to review their estimates. The focus fell on the hedged estimate on the development of the new technology. Surely the team did not need all that time. There must be some way to reuse an existing technology or find an outside firm with more and experienced resources to develop the technology. The project manager committed to explore those options while agreeing to commit to a nine-month project. In exchange, Marketing committed to work closely with the team and provide answers to the questions about the priority of the functionality. With that, the project started.

The engineering team felt confident they could develop and deliver, on time, the new technology. But, months went by with little progress on the technology. During status reports, engineering reported that they were turning the corner and would still meet their commitments. Marketing had not yet been able to dedicate resources to the team but would as soon as it looked as if engineering had turned the corner. In spite of this, the team remained committed to their date. Somehow, someway it would all come together. The message to the rest of the organization was that everything was on track. At the beginning of month eight, two months from the delivery date, reality hit the team. Engineering had finally figured out how to develop the new technology but it would take about six months to complete their work. Now that engineering knew how to approach the new technology, Marketing was finally ready to do the market research required. This was great news but it came way too late for the company to have any hope of meeting the nine-month commitment.

The focus of the team shifted to damage control. Now that they knew what was required to deliver the product, the team replanned the project and decided they could, this time with real confidence, deliver the project in six months. The bad news was that the product and sales would be late. The good news was that the product was actually viable. The project manager reported the slip in the date to the project sponsor. He was devastated. The sponsor had been telling the rest of the organization that all was well. Now, eight months into a nine-month project, the reality was a six-month delay. As he reported the bad news to the organization, as you might expect, he blamed the project manager and the team. The company dropped a task force on the project—partly to accelerate the project but mostly to find someone to blame.

Let me ask again, in view of this are we willing to consider using a different approach?

If not, how about this example?

At the start of the project, there was a lot we did not know:

- Would the required resources would be available when we needed them? Without these resources we would have to utilize external staff. But would the external resources be qualified to do the work?
- We were dependent on two projects that had to be done before we could complete our project. Would they both finish on time?
- Elements of our project depended on pending decisions about regulations. If those decisions were delayed, the project would be delayed. Depending on the decisions the regulators made, the project scope could change. When would the regulators issue their findings? What would their findings be? We had no idea.

In spite of a significant lack of knowledge, we had to make a commitment. We hedged as much as possible and padded our estimates as much as possible. We defined and documented a list of project caveats ("if—and we really mean if—the regulators delay their decision, our date will slip").

But we still had to make a commitment. There were simply too many others depending on us and our work. So we held our noses and gave a date that was then inscribed in stone. We worked hard to complete the tasks on time and compensate for the unavailability of resources but there was nothing we could do about those regulators. We explored contingencies that assumed different versions of the regulations but there were too many permutations to pursue.

During status meetings and updates, we reminded anyone who would listen about our caveats but that did not absolve us from the commitment we made—a commitment we made when we knew the least (does this sound familiar?). As our due date loomed, we pressed the regulatory agency for any insight into the regulations but the regulatory board was torn as to direction. We were stumped and stalled, as was the project.

The issue date for the regulations came and went and so did our project due date. Two months later, the agency issued a statement that they had decided to delay any decisions about the regulations—life would remain as it had been. With this unfinished decision finalized, we scrambled to finish the project. It was a great team that produced a great product but we were, at least temporarily, pariahs in the organization because we did not meet our commitment—a commitment we made when we knew the least. It was not our fault—but we had committed. What were we thinking?

Speaking for ourselves, we would rather try almost anything before we subject ourselves and our teams to the nearly always bad consequences of making a commitment when we know the least.

To only make commitments when we know enough and also to improve project performance, we developed a tool called Proactive Risk Management.

There are five steps in this approach:

1. Profile the risks to the project.
2. Quantify the risks to the project.
3. Define an acceptable level of risk before we commit to a date and deliverables.
4. Develop specific actions we will take to reduce the risks to the acceptable level.
5. Once we have reached the acceptable level of risk, make a commitment.

Let's go through each one.

1. Profile the Risks to the Project

There are many risk profiling models. We prefer to use a model we learned from Kent McDonald and Todd Little. In this model, there are three types of risks and two sources of risk. The types of risks include the following:

- Delivery risks—the risks of being late, over budget, and not on target.
- Business case risks—the risks that the case for the project is wrong. We deliver the project on time, on budget, and on target but it is the wrong project.
- Collateral damage risks—the unanticipated, negative ripple effects of the project. Perhaps our product scavenges other products in an unanticipated way.

For each of these types of risks, there are two sources of risks—uncertainty and complexity.

Uncertainty risks include, but *are not limited to*

- Market uncertainty
- Technical uncertainty
- Project duration
- Resource availability
- Domain knowledge availability
- Dependencies

Complexity risks include, but *are not limited to*

- Technical complexity
- Market segmentation and overlap
- Dependencies (the more there are, the more complex the project, the higher the risks)
- Team location (the more widely dispersed—even across organizational boundaries—the members of the team, the higher the complexity)
- Knowledge gaps (filling those gaps increases complexity)

Let's work through an example of profiling risks.

We needed to replace a fairly complex manual process with a new application. In the manual process, the sales team used a wide range of variables and intuition to match new customers to the appropriate salesperson. The members of the sales team were reasonable but adamant about building an application that exactly mimicked their complex manual process. In this case, our risk profile included a combination of delivery and business case risks. The sources of risk included

- **Technical uncertainty.** We were not sure how to develop technology to match human intuition and so creating such a technology included lots of uncertainty.
- **Process complexity.** In the manual process, a group of six salespeople spent three days per month mapping clients to salespeople based on client profile information. The process went through multiple iterations as the group sorted through variables such as salesperson load, area of specialization, geography, and likability (whatever that means).

- **Technical complexity.** Even forgetting about the technology that supports intuition, the rules engine to support the combination of matching variables was very complex.
- **Uncertainty about process standardization.** The sales team did not agree and could never agree on which of the variables should be the most important in matching a client to a salesperson.
- **Uncertainty about whether or not this project had any business value.** It would have been good to free up six members of the sales team for three days a month but did that compensate for the level of effort—both in the initial development and then through future enhancements and maintenance?

2. Quantify the Risks to the Project

With the risks profiled, we then needed to assess them so that we could determine which risks would keep us from both making a commitment and delivering a successful result.

In general, we can "score" the risks as a combination of impact and probability. If a risk would be devastating but is highly unlikely, we might assess this risk as being medium. If a risk is highly likely but has a low impact it, too, might be a medium risk. If a risk is both unlikely and has low impact, let's not worry about it. But if a risk has a high probability and a high impact, we want to focus on ways to reduce that risk.

Let's return to the example we started before. Our risks included:

- Technical uncertainty
- Process complexity
- Technical complexity
- Lack of standardization
- Business value uncertainty

Using a scale of 1 to 10, with 10 being high risk and 1 being low risk, we assessed these risks as shown in Table 7.1.

One way to visualize this risk assessment is using spider or radar diagrams. Figure 7.1 is the identical assessment but in a visual form.

This visualization helps us recognize where to focus our mitigation efforts. The biggest risk is in developing a technology to replicate the intuition of the sales team. Unless we can talk our sales team out of this idea or find a mind-reading technology, the project is at risk. We set ourselves up

Table 7.1   Risk Assessment

Risk	Assessment
Technical uncertainty	10
Process complexity	8
Technical complexity	7
Lack of standardization	6
Uncertainty about project value	8

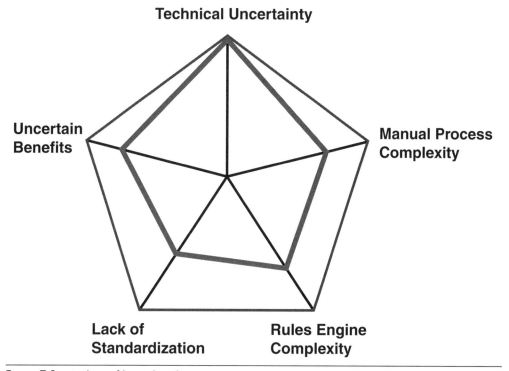

FIGURE 7.1   Risk profile radar diagram

for failure if we make a commitment as to timeline or functionality before we reduce this risk.

Now that we have profiled and assessed our risks, we know where to focus our efforts to reduce risk. As we reduce risk, we improve our chances for making and keeping commitments.

3. Define an Acceptable Level of Risk before We Commit to a Date and Deliverables

As a team and with our stakeholders and customers, we define and agree to an acceptable level of risk for each risk. From the profile and assessment, we know which are the high-priority risks. In order for this to work, we must have some level of consensus on what is an acceptable risk level. If engineering is incredibly risk averse but sales is more risk tolerant, this mismatch will drive frustration within both groups. Engineering will bemoan the cowboy attitude of those guys in sales. After all, don't they realize all of the bad things that can happen if things don't quite work as advertised? Sales will complain that the engineering team is taking too long to do the simplest things. But if both agree as to the risk profile, risk assessment, and acceptable level of risk, the project has a chance of success.

Working together, we determine how low each risk must be before we consider making a commitment. In our example, the process played out like this:

- **Technical uncertainty.** Sales wanted us to do something to capture their intuition. We told them we had no idea how to do that and offered to dissect what they called intuition to see if there was some underlying rule set we could uncover. When a salesperson felt that one client was a better match for a specific salesperson, what were the reasons? From this, we did identify a couple of previously undefined rules. Some of the intuition was based on the experience of the salesperson. No one wanted to match an inexperienced salesperson to an account with a spotted history. Another rule involved educational background. Some clients wanted a salesperson with at least a bachelor's degree. No one had ever formalized these rules but there they were. But even with these defined, there was still a need for a "gut feel" matching of salesperson to client. If technology could not support this, the risk would remain high. But could technology support most of the matching? Could we somehow use a set of known rules to propose a match that this group then used their intuition to confirm or change? If so, the risk level dropped dramatically. Would this combination of technology and manual review be acceptable? Would it handle enough of the matches to generate enough value? We decided to attach this to our iterative product development and try it out as part of our first phase. Doing this felt like an acceptable risk level of 5, a big decrease from the current level of 10.

- **Process complexity.** The current risk assessment gave this a risk score of 8. How low did we need to drive this risk level before we could commit? While there were some opportunities to simplify the process, we convinced ourselves that this would never be a straightforward process. Given that, we declared that moving from 8 to 6 would be acceptable.
- **Technical complexity.** Their matching process included quite a few variables. This resulted in a very complex rules engine design. Was there any possibility of reducing the number of variables? If so, the complexity would drop. With a drop in complexity, the risk, too, would drop. How low did it need to be? We agreed to a level of 3, down from 7 (which also motivated the team to find ways to reduce the rules engine complexity).
- **Lack of standardization.** This was going to be an issue no matter what we did and so we agreed that staying at a risk level of 6 was as good as we were going to get.
- **Uncertain value.** This one nagged me. Even if we created a wonderful product that did a perfect job of matching clients to salespeople, would it be worth the time, effort, and opportunity costs? What projects could we have done instead of working on this matching engine? The salespeople assured me that this product—if it worked—would be a home run. But how could we know for sure until we did the project and incurred the costs? Anytime benefits are uncertain, I like to validate the business case before we fully commit. I explained this approach to the team. We would develop an early, simple version of the matching product and then try it out on the matching process. We would monitor the benefits and extrapolate what they would be if we finished the product. Knowing this before we invested in the entire product would resolve some of our uncertainty. We agreed that we would revisit this risk after we had completed and tried out that first version. We said that the goal of this first version would be to get the acceptable risk from 8 to 5.

We drew this acceptable risk level on our radar diagram in green. Figure 7.2 shows the result.

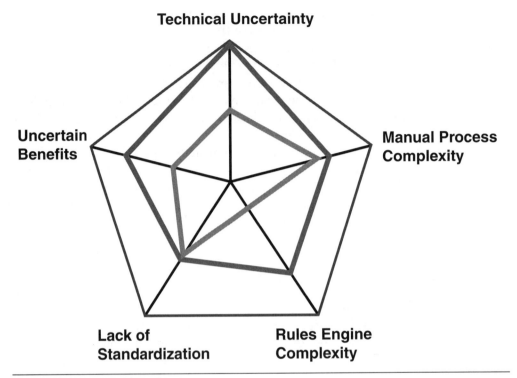

FIGURE 7.2   Acceptable risk

4. Develop Specific Actions We Will Take to Reduce the Risks to the Acceptable Level

Our conversations about what the risk levels must be before we commit had already yielded some concrete actions we could take to reduce the project risks. We added these steps into our project plans and backlog. Some of these actions are shown in Table 7.2.

With these risk-reducing actions front and center and very visible, we started the project. In the first iteration, we implemented our risk-reduction rules (develop rules only for which there is consensus) and the experience and education rules. We also gave ourselves some risk-reduction credit for deploying the first few, simple rules to reduce the risks of the complex rules engine. This changed our risk/commitment radar diagram as shown in Figure 7.3.

Table 7.2 Risk Mitigation Actions

Risk	Action Plans	When Deployed
Technical Uncertainty	No mind reading. Define rules for salesperson experience and education.	Experience and education rule in first iteration. Never deploy mind reading.
Manual Process Complexity	Deploy known rules and anticipate a final review for an intuition sanity check.	Prioritize rules development and testing in iteration planning. Stop when rules cannot be defined or when they add little value.
Rules Engine Complexity	Same as for Manual Process Complexity.	Same as for Manual Process Complexity.
Lack of Standardization	Develop rules only for which there is consensus. Sales team to reach consensus before including rules in iteration plans.	Immediately.
Uncertainty about Project Benefits	Consider each sprint a go/no-go gate. Pilot each sprint and evaluate the value of the last sprint before committing to the next iteration.	Immediately.

We still had to reduce the process complexity, rules engine complexity, and uncertain value risks before we could finalize any date or benefit commitments. And according to our action plans, we next needed to pilot what we had developed to see if there would be any actual value.

The sales team used this first version of the product at their next matchmaking meeting. With just a few simple rules in place, they shaved half a day off their meeting. Not huge but big enough to continue with the next iteration.

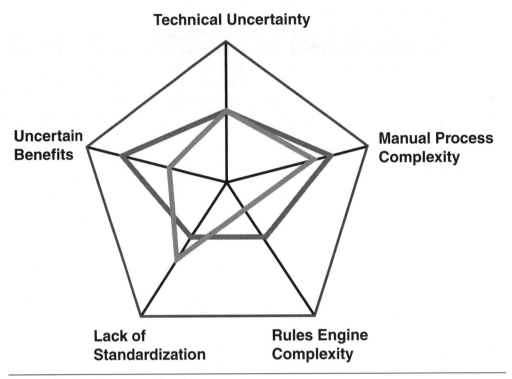

FIGURE 7.3   Iteration one risk profile

With some benefits now more certain, we updated our diagram as shown in Figure 7.4.

For the third iteration, the sales team agreed to some rules on vertical market and product experience. The team delivered the rules and then knew enough to architect the structure of a robust and variable rules engine. With that done, the risk profile changed to that shown in Figure 7.5.

Just one more pilot might get us inside all the acceptable risk levels—and able to make a solid commitment. This second pilot saved a full day from the matchmaking meeting—a significant and certain benefit. Figure 7.6 shows the resulting visual.

Along the way, we had made general commitments like: We will have the first iteration done by this date. After that, we will decide whether or not to move forward.

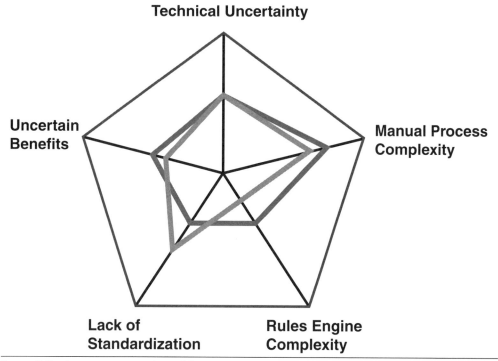

FIGURE 7.4   Iteration two risk profile

5. Once We Have Reached the Acceptable Level of Risk, Make a Commitment

Now, with two iterations and pilots complete, we were ready to discuss making commitments. We had a good idea as to the team velocity and pace. We had a good idea as to benefits. We could now commit to both dates and benefits. We still needed to manage the remaining work and make sure that we were not developing nebulous or overly complex rules or trying to read minds. In other words, we still had a big project to deliver but we were now able to make a commitment when we knew something.

"Purchasing" Options to Reduce Risks

There is another compelling advantage of using Proactive Risk Management. When we are brainstorming the actions we can take to reduce risks,

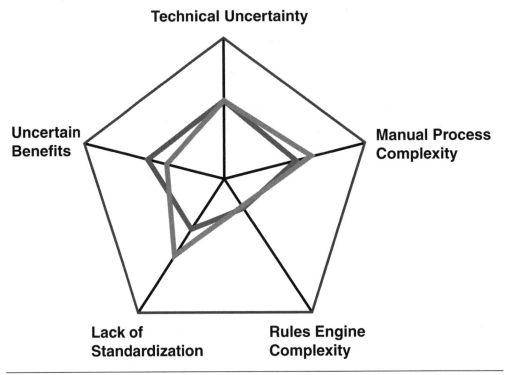

Technical Uncertainty

Uncertain Benefits

Manual Process Complexity

Lack of Standardization

Rules Engine Complexity

FIGURE 7.5   Iteration three risk profile

we can also identify actions or information we can "purchase" to reduce risks faster or sooner. For example, we might determine that we can, for a price, allocate a person from the team to do a deep investigation of—perhaps even set up and run—a new technology. This might cost us the work of that one team member, but if doing so quickly gets a yes or no answer regarding technical uncertainty, it might be well worth the price. Once we have profiled the risks, risk-reduction options are more visible.

We were doing a large and critical analytics project. This project would predict customer retention based on a relatively small set of parameters. If this project worked, we would know which customers were trending away for us. Knowing this, we could then do an intervention to retain those customers. As a second phase of the project, we could categorize customers into their *potential* for leaving us and do things, proactively, to make sure they never even started to trend away from us. But this entire predictive

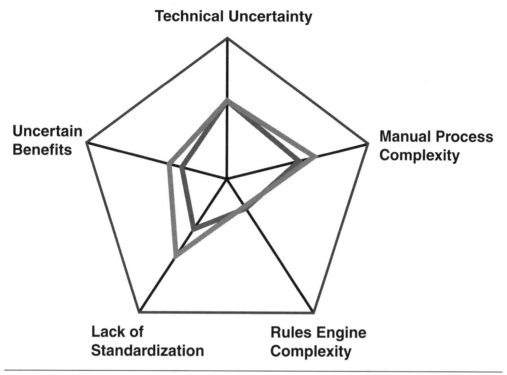

FIGURE 7.6   Iteration four risk profile

model assumed we had access to information about our customers that we simply did not collect. Thus, the enabler of this entire project came down to gathering that information. To make matters worse, there was no single way to collect the data.

As a team, we brainstormed various methods we could use to get this information. We identified four ways that would cause the least pain and two ways that would cause us to make big changes across our systems. Always wanting the easiest way out, we agreed to try the four less painful methods. Given the critical nature of this project, we agreed to pursue all four in parallel. In effect, we "paid" for parallel development as a way to reduce project uncertainty as quickly as possible. We allocated a team to each method and set them free. And, for once, we got it right. Information for some customers was available with only one method while information for different types of customers came via a different method.

Paying the "price" of parallel development reduced our project uncertainty sooner than a serial approach would have done.

Proactive Risk Management works extremely well if we get close to the truth when we profile the risks, are realistic about the actions we can take to reduce the risks to an acceptable level, somehow resist the pressure to make commitments until we know enough, and make it all visible to everyone—including the people who want that premature commitment.

Making Proactive Risk Management Visible

Proactive Risk Management is not only a way to consciously mitigate risks while taking a more sensible approach to commitment making, it is also a powerful management tool for tracking team progress and communicating status and success—by making them visible.

We can sum up our passion for making everything visible with the following motto:

It is better to see than it is to read.

What does that mean? It means that we should find ways to make all of our work more picture dense than word dense. In fact, making work visual is one of the fundamental principles of iterative development. Using iterative principles, we prefer working software to comprehensive documentation. Why? Because no one knows what they want until they "see" it, and they can read but can't "see" requirements documents.

This ability to "see" is critical in Proactive Risk Management. Imagine the power of a set of risk level/acceptable risk level radar diagrams on a project dashboard. In the set, we show how we are iterating toward risks being at the acceptable level and our being able to make a specific commitment. Such a visual shows not only our commitment-making target but also that we have profiled the risks and implemented a plan that proactively reduces these risks, all at a glance.

Let's apply this to our method of Proactive Risk Management. Imagine the power of a visual that shows the risk profile radar diagrams, the level of acceptable risk (prior to making a commitment), and the progress the team is making toward acceptable risk and commitment making. For a project dashboard, consider a series of these radar diagrams that demonstrate your progress. In the preceding example, we showed our progress with a series of radar diagrams that marked the shrinking risk. Figure 7.7 shows how we iterated toward acceptable risk.

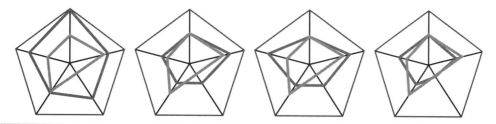

FIGURE 7.7   Risk mitigation progress

Naturally, the information we use to create the visual reports must be accurate and complete. Where does that information come from? It comes from the various teams. But how can we find a balance between accurate and complete information and burdensome status reporting? To be honest, that is a balance that you will have to find for yourself and your teams.

Make Progress Visible

In one of my turnaround CIO roles, I inherited an IT team that had no credibility in the organization. As you can imagine, IT morale was low and turnover was high. As I talked with IT's stakeholders and customers, one message came through loud and clear—IT never gets anything done. This attitude was so pervasive that the organization actively looked for ways to not use the internal IT department. If something required a connection to a legacy system, the project sponsor would reluctantly include the IT group. But if the project could stand on its own, the project was even more appealing since there was no need to tie the project deliverables to the boneheads in IT.

In truth, the IT department was highly skilled. There were clearly issues with priorities—which we improved using iterative principles and methods—but we got the biggest bang by using visual displays to communicate the status and completion of projects. One of the things we technical types do really poorly is communicate our work. One of the sad truths about human nature is this:

In the absence of communication, we assume the worst.

If we do not clearly and simply communicate the status of a project, people will assume there is not progress. The only way to change this is to communicate. The best way to communicate is visually.

Returning to my story, as we held project demos and iterative planning sessions, we recorded, at a lightweight and high level, the status and plans for each and every major project. Every two weeks, we turned this information into a report that we sent to the entire organization. The format of the report was a series of swim lanes—one lane for each project. The lane contained the high-level information about what was already complete, what was in progress, and what was planned. The chart did not include the in-release or in-sprint details. Rather, it provided a status at the product level. Figure 7.8 is an example of how we made our projects and their progress visual.

Every two weeks, it took about 30 minutes to update and distribute this report. Those 30 minutes every other week completely changed the organization's perception of the IT group. When the organization could quickly and easily see (but not have to read) what projects were active, their status, and their completion, everyone in the organization decided we knew what we were doing and were good at what we were doing. Had we tried to communicate this same information is a wordy spreadsheet or text-heavy document, few would have read the report or understood the flow of the work (complete, in progress, planned). The visual nature of the information allowed people, at a glance, to not only know what was going on but also that we were good at delivery. Remember, when it comes to communication, **It is better to see than it is to read.**

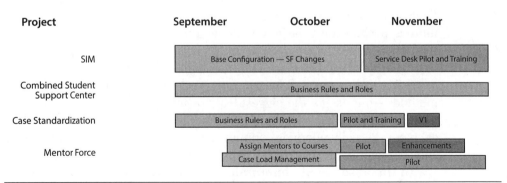

FIGURE 7.8   Project swim lanes

When we first determined we had to use information to change the perception of IT's ability, we struggled with how to capture the relevant information. In our first attempt, we created a shared document and asked each team lead to update their project status. This worked reasonably well in terms of gathering the right information but it was a nightmare to compile into a higher-level, consolidated report we could distribute. Next, we tried an every-other-week, face-to-face meeting with all of the teams. We hoped this meeting would not only surface the information we needed but also identify any cross-team coordination and dependencies. This worked well for the dependency management but was too frequent for any major changes in coordination. In terms of status reporting, it generated the information we needed but at the expense of consuming too many people's time for too long. So after a two tries, we scrapped the meeting and tried something else.

Previously, I had had good success with what I called a 3P report. Those 3Ps are Progress, Plans, and Problems. Every two weeks, the teams reported what they had finished (Progress), what they would get done in the next two weeks (Plans), and any issues they needed leadership to resolve (Problems). Done correctly, this approach not only provides status information but also provides some tracking—if all is going well, the Plans in the current report should show up as Progress in the next report. But, this method can also become onerous if the reports take too much time to complete and compile. For my IT group, this method worked the best. I told each team to take no more than five minutes to create their report. Every other week, I would compile that information and translate it into our swim lane format. It all worked without too much pain—at least until something better came along. And nothing better came along. The swim lane was so useful and popular that every project in the company soon showed up in swim lane form.

Ambiguity and Iterative Methods

When using iterative methods we accept either that we do not yet know everything or that the future is uncertain—perhaps both. Rather than selecting a path and sticking to it—no matter how the environment changes around us—we take a series of small steps. At the end of each step, we evaluate the next steps we should take in order to get to the final destination.

In practice, by delivering iteratively, the customer and the team evaluate the business value of the product and determine, based on newly available knowledge, if it is best to adjust. Done well, iterative methods have proven successful for the teams that have used them.

In one company I worked at, we decided to experiment with iterative methods, but we wanted to put the iterative approach to a real test. We had one software project that was, after six months of intense development, six months behind schedule. The team was developing an entirely new version of one of our legacy products. There were lots of opinions about the product direction and required functionality. There was also a lot of uncertainty: Which features were the most important? What should the user interface look like? Which back-end technologies should we use?

The product requirements changed almost daily. For every step the team took forward, something pushed them backward. The team felt they were on a death march with no chance for success. They worked hard every day but never got anything done. The team's customer was incredibly frustrated (even though it was this customer that, in grappling with all of the unknowns, continually changed the requirements). We figured that this project was the perfect candidate for our experiment with iterative methods. After all, if the new approach did not work, what was the downside? We deliver an even worse complete failure?

We trained the team in the basics of iterative development and spent a lot of time explaining the approach to the team's customer. We did the high-level planning and prioritization, then planned the first iteration and did some medium-level planning of a couple of the following iterations. Everyone committed to keep the requirements in the current iteration completely solid—no one could change their minds or introduce new features or change the priority. If there were any changes, the team would deal with those in the future iterations. It took several cycles for everyone to become proficient at this approach but the team was soon generating real, valuable, working software at the end of each iteration. The team's customer settled into her role and soon became a staunch advocate for not making any in-iteration changes. Instead, she focused on defining the next phase of the future work. At the end of each iteration, we collected feedback, learned, and adjusted. What was the result? In just six week (yes, weeks), a project that had been six months behind schedule was back on schedule.

Now, these results are not typical and your actual results may vary but the message is clear. If you are dealing with uncertainty—uncertainty about anything—iterative methods work much better than mapping and sticking to a path that does not recognize that things will change.

In Summary

We like to sum up the role of project management this way:

Once the planning is over and the project is under way, only bad things can happen.

All of these bad things are risks to the project. Rather than waiting for the bad things to happen, we should profile and prioritize the risks during project planning. We can then build risk mitigation into our plans and proactively manage the risks. This approach not only improves project performance, it also allows us to deal with the commitment tension—the pressure to make commitments when we know the very least. This also helps leaders understand the multitude of reasons we cannot commit to a date—yet.

Finally, making our risk mitigation visible not only helps our stakeholders understand why we cannot yet make detailed commitments, it also helps us promote our progress.

Because it is nearly impossible to predict the future, we are awash in ambiguity. Rather than defining a project plan that assumes no modifications, we should define our future state but take small steps toward that future state—pausing at the end of each step to reevaluate the new conditions before we take the next step.

CHAPTER 8

Tools to Deal with Walls

The Big Ideas

- There will be barriers between us and getting to Energy and Innovation.
- There will be resistance to change.
- Focus on value not dates, manage up, and learn how to collaborate with non-collaborators.

It's Hard

I sometimes think life would be so much easier if people would stop getting in the way. Sadly, that is rarely the case. If we are in any type of leadership position, we deal with people. And, at an organizational level, we deal with the organization's culture. At the core, it takes collaboration to move teams or the organization from point A to point B. Ideally, we do this by creating a compelling and shared vision so that our teams and organizations, willingly and passionately, will move to point B. In reality, we might encounter people and a culture that are reluctant or hesitant to go along. This becomes a barrier that we must deal with, one we may come up against again and again.

We might hear things like the following:

- Why should we do anything differently? Things seem to be just fine.
- This sounds like another one of those management fads.
- I am tired of change. Just leave me alone.
- If the leaders are not on board, I am not going to do anything.
- That sounds nice but will never work here.

Sometimes these walls come from rigid, unforgiving processes and rules.

What can we do about such "walls"? In this chapter, we present several tools that might be useful when you encounter a wall.

"I Need It by This Date! And I Need It All!"

Has this ever happened to you? You are tasked with leading the project that will create the company's next killer product or that will replace that nagging legacy system or that will finally allow the company to analyze product and customer trends. Your marching orders are very clear—the project must be done by March 15. With the date fixed, you plan the project. You identify tasks, resources, costs, dependencies, and technologies and lay out a schedule. You manipulate tasks, resources, costs, dependencies, and technologies to achieve the project goal of hitting the required date.

When you meet with your project sponsor and stakeholders, are their questions all about the likelihood hitting that date? Whether intentionally or unintentionally, all things become subservient to hitting that date. Each time a dependency is late or a technology does not immediately work as advertised, you have to make project trade-offs. But the one thing you have learned is that you will not be able to trade off that date. So, you reduce the scope a bit and then a lot—whatever it takes to hit that date. Some things fall your way and, as the project nears its due date, you can, with confidence, claim that you will hit that all-important date. True, the project is different from what you first planned but you will hit your date. Your sponsor is relieved. Your stakeholders sing your praises. The product launches, the legacy system limps to the boneyard, and the analysis provides some insight. But the product does not do as well, the new system does not perform as well, the analysis of product and customer trends is not as revealing because, in order to hit that date, you had to make a few sacrifices—in some cases a lot of sacrifices. You did the best you could but because the date became the most important deliverable, you designed around the date—even if that required you to suboptimize the product, the system, or the analysis.

What about a different approach? We start the project the traditional way with a hard and fast due date. The project is a major—and innovative—upgrade of our customer portal. As we gather and sort through the high-level requirements, we ask, over and over again, what are we trying to achieve with this upgrade? How will we know that the project has delivered value? What are the drivers behind each required element of the upgrade? Who will use that piece of functionality and what do they want to accomplish? How would they benefit from the upgrade?

Taking this more customer-focused approach to the project changes the conversation and the insistence on meeting a specific date. To be sure, hitting a date still matters but delivering the desired value to our customers is the primary goal. As the project progresses, we make the traditional scope, time, and cost trade-offs but we make trade-offs that either retain or improve the value to our customers. In addition, our customer-value perspective encourages us and our sponsor to interact frequently with our customers—through a series of focus groups and product demonstrations—in order to determine which features and functions provide the most value. As we prioritize our work, the high-impact features float to the top and become the focus of what we will get done first. It turns out that our customers have a burning desire to know, in incredible detail, the status of their orders. It also turns out that some of the features we think are really cool and bleeding edge are just not that interesting to our customers.

When the project ends, we assess our performance. We delivered early the functionality that made the biggest difference to our customers and to the company. By continuously focusing on what creates customer value, we found the shortest, most direct path to customer value. As part of this ongoing prioritization we did not develop some of the features and functions that were originally planned—why build something our customers told us they did not really need or want?

But from a completely objective view, we were "late" with some of the low-priority features. Does this mean that the project was challenged? Only if the goal were to hit a date first and worry about value second.

As twisted as this logic sounds, how often is this our thought process? How often is a date how we define accomplishment? And, if this is common, let's agree to stop doing so right now and focus on value first.

This focus on due dates will be one of the biggest walls you will hit. And you will come up against it again and again.

In real life there is always significant pressure to deliver the maximum value to the business and to our customers. This is evidenced by business managers demanding a long list of detailed requirements by a specific date. How do we deal with it? We need to understand the real issues and how best to respond to them.

The issue is a classic one:

- The business needs the maximum delivery.
- The development team has limited resources and time.
- The effort required is uncertain.

How do we deal with this reality? The business must deliver as much value as possible but it is the development team that actually does the work with limited resources. Without goodwill and cooperation this often leads to unhelpful and wasteful conflict between the business areas instead of focusing on problems as a whole business.

How can we avoid this?

Start by collaborating to understand and accept the dynamics and the reality of the situation.

- The business needs the maximum that can be delivered.
- Both business and development teams are well intentioned and motivated to do the best that they can.
- There is essentially a fixed set of resources and time available.
- Because the effort is uncertain, we don't know exactly what can be done.
- If we overload the delivery team, they will be demotivated and deliver less than they might and at a lower quality than we want.

Iterative approaches help take the pressure out of the situation and enable maximum delivery.

- Jointly focus on cash flow and speed to market rather than on some theoretical plan.
- Get the cash flow going by delivering the minimal viable product as quickly as possible.
- Prioritize. Create the product incrementally, tackling the highest-value items first.
- Have the business and development leaders work together to enable increased effectiveness in the engineering team.
- The business must be available for quick decision making when needed.

- Invest in making the infrastructure and process as supportive as possible.
- Remove interruptions.
- Minimize unhelpful reviews.
- Focus on delivery.

The foundation of dealing with this is a genuine *partnership* between business areas and development teams. A senior leader's primary goal should be to jointly build a collaborative vision and alignment across the whole organization.

Managing Up

I once worked with a team that was not meeting their weekly commitments—consistently. I wondered why. Their work was always good when they did deliver. So I stopped by their work area.

"How is it going?" I asked. "You seem to be struggling with your weekly commitments. What is getting in your way?"

There was a pause. "Mr. Shore comes by and keeps giving us new tasks to do," the team leader replied.

"You don't stop everything and do them, do you?"

"Well, yes. We are going to work for him when this project is over!"

I now understood the problem and walked up to Mr. Shore's office. "I know you are worried about getting the things built you will need in the future. And we will get them all done. Give us a list and the team will prioritize what they will do every week and they will deliver." He did and the team was back on track.

A command and control manager is very difficult to deal with—but not impossible. As a team leader, if you have such a manager, you can manage up and protect the team. Or the team may select a leader from their team to manage this micromanager. How do they do this?

First, find out what is important to your manager and why. Most likely he wants control and certainty but how does he get them? Collecting metrics no one actually uses? Having people do it "his way"? Seeing progress on a daily or weekly basis? Measuring against a plan? Is he afraid of failure? In this situation, what can you do?

Generate Data

Somehow micromanagers think that collecting data will assure them that things are working. Whether the data is really useful or not, they still want it. The essential part is to not waste the team's time. As the team's leader, you need to minimize the impact on the team by gathering the data and creating the report, just as your controlling manager wants it. Protect the team.

"Do It My Way"

Use the Macro-Leadership Cube in Chapter 5, Ownership Tools, either as a drawing or a mental image. With your micromanager, identify and agree to the constraints and expected results but in quantitative terms. For example, it is not enough to have an expected result as increase sales. It must be by how much sales will increase. Five percent? Eight percent? Then ask the manager to step back as long as the team operates within the boundaries of the expected results and any constraints. As a first step, make sure the team agrees with the possible cube constraints and expected results before you talk to the manager.

Show Progress

Building an electronic stock exchange was a massive project. The project leader, Mr. Smith, was not technical so he focused on interfacing with the clients. After all, there were over 50 banks paying for the exchange, some very large and some very small. They all wanted their say.

I took the helm to deliver the product. After a close look at the effort, I realized that using waterfall methods would not cut it. There was way too much uncertainty to be able to accurately project the tasks and completions. We needed something else and the *team* figured it out. They started an iterative development process. The team designed, coded, and tested small bits of functionality and showed them to customers. The customers gave feedback and we adjusted accordingly.

However, Mr. Smith wasn't technical. The only thing he knew about software delivery was to use waterfall methods. On such a high-risk project, was he willing to go for an experimental "made up" methodology like iterative development?

I wasn't sure how well he would accept our approach and so I built a high-level waterfall chart. This chart had three of the familiar waterfall phases: design, develop, and test. I spread these three phases across the two-and-a-half-year project lifecycle. In the background, the development team continued to deliver small bits of functionality, fully tested, once a week, continuously integrating the bits daily and hardening the system every three months. I mapped this progress onto the appropriate phase on the waterfall chart.

I discovered that Mr. Smith often came into the office on Sunday afternoon to do his paperwork. I started going into the office on Sunday afternoons to have casual conversations about the project. Together, we would look at the waterfall chart. During the waterfall design phase, I would explain to him all of the design work we had done and were doing. During the development phase, I would describe all of the development that was done and under way. Same with the testing phase. And, because we were always doing design, development, and testing—I could truthfully tell him how what we were doing mapped to his preferred, comfortable, waterfall way.

He wanted to see progress—against his waterfall plan—and I showed him progress as he could understand it.

One of the ways to manage up is to translate your work into terms your micromanager understands.

Check In Often

Micromanagers want information, so give it to them. Let your micromanager know what is going on regularly. Find the best format for this: e-mail, reports, stopping by his office. Then talk about what the team has accomplished and what they are working on for the near future. Make sure that the team is pretty confident they can deliver on the tasks coming up. If you have issues, explain how you are solving them.

Collaborating with Non-Collaborators

"Steve, what are you doing here?" Steve was the leader of the workstation team for the stock exchange.

"You know why."

"Actually, I don't have a clue. What's up?"

"If you don't get John off the team, the team will throw him out the window."

Okay. That sounded serious. After four prototypes on the user interface, John had volunteered to write the specification so other teams could develop the back end. Seemed straightforward to me.

"What happened?" I asked.

"Well, he wrote the spec but he didn't write it based on the final prototype. He has written it on what *he* wanted the interface to look like." In other words, the team had lost six weeks on an already tight schedule.

John is a typical non-collaborator. He decided to act on his own, fully independent from the rest of the team. Not only that, he was, in general, tough to work with.

When we think about moving from where we are and into Energy and Innovation, it is highly likely we will encounter walls—barriers that either slow us down or block us on our journey. And, no doubt about it, one of the most common and significant walls you will hit will be people who don't want to change, who don't want to collaborate. From the previous chapters and our own experience, we know that to create the high-trust, high-ownership, innovative culture we want, collaboration is key.

Non-collaborators can be both persons and processes. Non-collaborators come in many versions: people who resist new ideas that are not their own; like things the "way they are"; want it "their way" or no way; want to be the lone hero; are unfocused; or do not believe in the purpose. These human non-collaborators exhibit behaviors such as being disruptive or rude, withholding information the team needs, committing to one thing and doing another, working in isolation, and knowing it all.

Likewise, non-collaborators can be processes that require blind obedience, cause churn, burden teams, impose unnecessary work and effort, and promote process over results. Non-collaborators are difficult to work with—but not impossible.

How do we collaborate with non-collaborators? In this section, we offer techniques to collaborate with the non-collaborators you will inevitably encounter as you make your way up toward a healthy, energetic, and innovative culture. First, through an assessment process, you will gain insights on your non-collaborators to narrow down the techniques that you could use to collaborate with them. To figure out how to work with them, an understanding of what makes them tick will come in handy. Finally, what about you? Why do you want to work with these people and what risks are you willing to take? After all, something could go terribly wrong and you might be humiliated, isolated, demoted, and possibly lose your job.

With this information in hand, we look at several general techniques that help you work with many non-collaborators. Finally, with the help of our Trust-Ownership Model in Chapter 2, Trust and Ownership, the traits of your non-collaborators are mapped to this model to provide specific techniques for dealing with your non-collaborators.

Think of a Non-Collaborator

I bet that didn't take long. It seems like there is always at least one. Is your non-collaborator your manager? A team member? Another team? Or a process?

A non-collaborating process is a process that keeps people from collaborating. For example, a stack-ranked, independent performance review system. If my raise depends on how high I am in the stack, I might not help others succeed and move up in the stack ahead of me. And I want the credit for my accomplishments; I don't want others to have it. That's not encouraging collaboration.

So, non-collaborators can appear anywhere in your organization.

Assessment

The collaborating with non-collaborators process starts by assessing your non-collaborator and looking at your motivation and risks in collaborating. We will first focus on the non-collaborator as a person or team, the more common type. Later, we talk about dealing with non-collaborative processes (a whole separate kettle of fish). This is followed by a separate section for assessing why you want to collaborate with this non-collaborator, what you are willing to risk, and how collaborative you are.

The assessment has many parts, so we have included a worksheet for you in Appendix D, Collaborating with Non-Collaborators Worksheet. In the meantime, let's start the process.

Non-Collaborator Traits

I am sure you haven't forgotten your non-collaborator. How do you know she is a non-collaborator? Does she have any of the following traits?

- Obstructive
- Hard to reach
- Won't attend meetings
- Finger pointing
- Not consistent
- Can't be trusted
- Misses the big picture
- Narrow world/company view
- Self-promoting
- Ladder climber
- Has own agenda
- Passive (no initiative)
- Lack of interest
- Lack of participation
- Doesn't listen to others' ideas
- Negative
- Manipulative
- Bureaucratic
- Nonsupportive
- Inflexible
- Dismissive
- Unkind
- Stubborn
- Difficult
- Argumentative
- Resists change
- Defers decisions
- Deflects
- Disrespectful
- Combative
- Confrontational
- Demagogic
- Selfish
- Takes credit for others' ideas
- Knows everything
- Avoids accountability
- Problem avoidance
- Doesn't work with the team
- Not willing to help others
- Works alone
- Defensive
- "That's not my job"
- Doesn't complete work
- Their way only
- Withholds information
- Self-serving
- Unwilling to compromise
- Does not follow the process
- Blames others
- "Can't do" attitude

Now you have a better description of how your non-collaborator behaves.

Types of Non-Collaborators

It seems that most non-collaborators fall into three categories:

- They don't know how to collaborate.
- They are afraid to collaborate.
- "It's all about me!" They think collaboration reduces their power and influence.

There may be more but these seem to be the most common. Let's take a closer look at each of these.

Many times people don't know how to collaborate. Or their experience has *taught* them *not* to collaborate. They don't know even where to start or with whom they should collaborate. They might not trust the people they need to collaborate with.

Sometimes it is difficult to tell if they don't know how or they are afraid to collaborate. In the workplace, people can fear many things—real or not. Common fears are losing control, failure, looking foolish or unqualified, and someone else taking credit for your ideas and successes. And in today's economy, everyone worries about losing their jobs. This can be a risk if we are not seen to be adding value or if we lose control and fail. Other fears include discovering your new boss is a micromanager, landing in a career-limiting position, or being shut out of the inner circle.

Warren Bennis, one of the definitive pioneers in the contemporary field of leadership, reports that in collaboration people fear three things: losing their identity, losing their intellectual mastery, and losing their individualism [1].

As an example of fear affecting collaboration, in a stack-ranked performance review system, people fear if they collaborate, someone else with get the credit for something great they did. You can see the damaging effect fear can have.

Now we come to the non-collaborator I see the most, the "It's all about me!" person. Not only are they difficult to deal with, they are difficult to like. Arrogance goes hand in hand with a huge ego. They not only feel they are superior to others, they *know* they are! They can be quite brilliant sometimes but at other times they just think they are. They have little or no self-awareness. They have a strong personal agenda: Their way is the best way for the company, when often it is not. It's "my way or the highway" when dealing with them. Because their way is the best, they must achieve it. To do this they want power and control. They don't ask for it, they take it. In other words, they *must* win.

They always want their fingers in anything under the spotlight. We taught collaborative leadership in a large company and Doris loved it. She became a trainer and brought the course to her entire division. But when she attended the Collaborating with Non-Collaborators course, she hated it and her evaluation showed it.

"How come Doris didn't like the class?" the training coordinator asked.

"She's a non-collaborator," I answered.

"But she loves collaborating and collaborative leadership."

"When does Doris collaborate?" I asked.

She thought a moment. "Only when the project is in the spotlight. The rest of the time, she doesn't collaborate."

"Correct."

Often these non-collaborators are passive-aggressive, someone who is supportive and agreeable in discussion, yet after they leave the room they are negative and dishonest. They are polite, then suddenly angry. They come late to meetings to maintain control over the group. Obstructionist, victim attitude, always makes excuses, and difficult to pin down are all traits of a passive-aggressive person.

Enough about them. I am certain you have run across one of the "all about me" non-collaborators at least once in your life. When I think of a typical non-collaborator, I think of Dan. He had every one of the characteristics mentioned earlier: He knew what was best for the company; he had so many ideas and spent hours explaining them to everyone who would listen; he assumed he had power, yet he never committed to delivering on his ideas, or if he did, he never delivered any results. He withheld information to gain control and keep his power. He could do one thing and one thing well. When the company let him only do that in isolation, he left, much to the relief of everyone who had tried to work with him.

What Makes Your Non-Collaborator Tick?

Why does your non-collaborator do what he does? Why does a team behave the way they do? Well, if we knew the answers, dealing with him or the team would be much easier. However, with human beings, such things are difficult to know. We might get a sense of what drives him by looking at what actions he takes at work and how he views the world. Any insights you gain might shed some light on how you can collaborate with him.

When you answer the questions that follow, rely on what you *think* the answer might be. Your first reaction is often the right call. And you don't need to be exact. All you need is a reasonable picture of how your non-collaborator sees and deals with the world, especially the work environment.

Motivation is the first place to look. What seems to get him excited about a project or an idea? How does he define success? Is it financial? Or job satisfaction? Along that line, how is he rewarded? And slightly differently, what recognition and acknowledgement does he want? What topics or initiatives in your organization is he interested in? Where is his focus?

Hidden agendas can be very difficult to deal with because they do not align with the purpose of the organization (thus, they are hidden). You might not be able to figure out what the agenda is but you should be able to detect whether he has one or not.

What is his leadership style? If you are dealing with someone who controls or micromanages, and you are a collaborative leader, be aware that your non-collaborator will likely push you. You must remain calm and ignore it.

Does he participate in company politics? Is he on a career path at the expense of the organization's goals? And if so, who does he see as his competition? Is he a loner in the organization or does he have allies? And is he trusted by others above him and around him? Or below him?

Finally, what fears does he have? Fear of failure? Lack of recognition? Loss of power and control? Looking stupid? What do you see?

Why Do You Want to Collaborate?

I was facilitating a group of managers at an off-site meeting when one manager, David, rattled off a list of decisions he had made that affected the entire group. The silence in the room was deafening. "Well," I said to the group, "There's David, collaborating with himself again." Everyone laughed, including David.

What are the reasons you want to collaborate with your non-collaborator? What is motivating you? How much are you willing to risk to make the collaboration work? These are all useful questions to help you deal more effectively with your non-collaborator.

Let's take a closer look. What are you passionate about? What turns your lights on when you get to try something or do something? What projects at work make you want to come to work? Along with that, what do you do best? Are you good at mentoring, coaching, managing projects, teaching, doing? Most important, how do *you* define success? Making a difference in an organization, being an influencer, moving up the corporate ladder, a fancy title on a business card, a certain figure salary? What is important to you? Finally, what are your fears?

What about the differences between you and your non-collaborator? On the scales in Figure 8.1, mark where your non-collaborator sits and where you sit. For example, in the first scale, how far are they from the total non-collaborator end? How far are you from the total collaborator

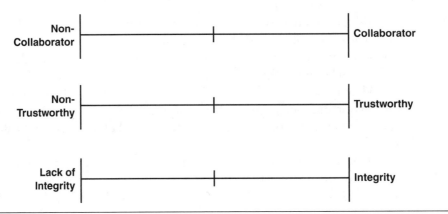

FIGURE 8.1   Collaboration, Trust, and Integrity scales

end? Do the same for the scales on trust and integrity. We talked about their importance in Chapter 2, Trust and Ownership.

You need to be clear about why you want to collaborate with this non-collaborator. What is *your* agenda? Is it for a business reason? Do you need information or actions so you or your team can succeed? Do you need your non-collaborator to stand back? You want to *change* your non-collaborator? While this last option might be your agenda, it is not likely you can change another person. You can only change processes or the way *you* interact with the non-collaborator.

Your Risks

How much are you willing to risk in trying to collaborate with your non-collaborator? If it doesn't work out, you could risk losing your job or being demoted. Okay, that does sound drastic. However, it might happen.

On a less drastic level, you could lose respect from people and their trust. You might be moved out of the inner circle or be placed in the penalty box. You might be able to recover from this over time but you may also be limiting your advancement possibilities. Is dealing with the non-collaborator that important to you?

Do you care if someone else takes the credit for your ideas? This may matter if you are under stack ranking in your independent performance review.

What are your risks? Can you

- Survive without your mentors?
- Let someone else take the credit for your ideas and accomplishments?
- Deal with any undeserved, negative labels?
- Deal with public humiliation?
- Handle your career being derailed in this organization?
- Handle being fired?
- Find another job as good or better within three months?

As you decide, consider all the successful risks you have taken in the past.

What Will You Do?

Do you think your non-collaborator will ever engage in collaboration? Or do you need to work around them?

Let's look at the first option: he will at least respond to your efforts to collaborate. There are general techniques to help and there are techniques for specific cases.

Let's start with the general techniques first.

General Techniques for Dealing with Non-Collaborators

When dealing with non-collaborators, communication, the content of the communication, and the way you deliver the communication can all be misconstrued. I have divided the techniques into these three categories with techniques for each category.

Communication

The language you use, the frequency of communicating, and your intent are important. Remember, your non-collaborator might be tuning you out, so extra effort needs to be made so she can hear you.

Speak So You Can Be Heard

"My developers don't know how to communicate!" one manager said to me.

"Did you hire them to communicate?" I replied. "Would you like to send them to a communications course or have them write code?"

The answer seems obvious. When people are going on and on and the language seems more and more obscure, that's when you need to pay attention. They have something important to say. Listen carefully. Learn to hear their language and speak it back to them.

Once I tried this with a non-collaborator and every time I would get close to understanding enough to talk to her, she changed the subject. I would set about trying again only to have her change the subject again. She was a brilliant woman but eventually left the company because people stopped talking to her.

Use a language your non-collaborator understands. Remember what is important to your non-collaborator from the questions you answered earlier in this section.

Communicate Often

And over communicate. State everything you know about the topic. When information is withheld, people are angry and afraid. Say everything and watch for signals that enough has been said. Check in with your non-collaborator on a regular basis so he knows where things are.

Practice a Forward-Going Approach

Don't wait for your non-collaborator to come to you. Go to him. When I worked with a marketing team for an online shopping company, the marketers always wondered what was coming next from the web developers. "Just ask them," I answered. "They're sitting on the other side of the room."

Content

What you are saying matters. What is most important is value to your business and value to your customers. Don't communicate only the problems, come with a few possible solutions or pathways to getting to a solution. Finally, share all the information you can. Be transparent.

Focus on Business Value

"We need some help! Everyone is working like crazy, a lot of overtime at night and on the weekends. We need another person on the team." I was desperate. As team leader, I was watching the team work harder and harder to get their work done, wearing themselves out, losing motivation, and beginning to make errors that caused more time in rework.

"What do you mean? The work always gets done. I thought software teams always worked that way." That was the manager's response.

I was floored. I didn't understand. Then I realized I hadn't helped my manager understand. He had a budget and his budget was tight. So I did my time-to-benefit for him. I showed how much sooner the project would generate the benefits if we added another resource to the team. The costs of the additional resources were so much smaller than the benefits of accelerating the project schedule. But until I spoke in the language that he understood (return on investment, time to benefit, business value), he saw only the additional and unacceptable costs. When presented with the data in his terms, he approved the new hire.

Delivering value to the market is the main reason we do business, but it is not a mathematical calculation. It is a conversation. Speak in terms of business model, time to value, revenue gain, and cost reductions. We can't deliver products and services alone.

Bring Solutions, Not Just Problems

"Hi, Chris. How's it going?" I had stopped by the coffee room for a minute. Even though I was an executive on the project, no one worried about telling me what I needed to know.

"Okay, but how long do we need to keep covering for George? It's been three months and he is still learning."

Oh, no, I thought. This is a critical member of a critical key team. We knew it was complicated to bring a new person onto the team—difficult enough that we estimated it would take about six weeks for someone to contribute to the team. With George, this time had at least doubled. Rather than answer Chris, I waited.

"Is there another place in the organization for him?" Chris continued. "He is a talented guy and he has learned a lot about the system. He's just not the right fit for our team."

I trusted Chris. He was a talented developer and a loyal team member, very committed to the success of the project. If Chris said he wasn't the right fit, he wasn't the right fit. After all, his team had picked George to work with them. I found another place in the organization for George and got a replacement for him on Chris's team. All worked well. Rather than just present a problem, Chris provided a solution—move George to a team where he would be a better fit.

When people come to my office with problems and no solutions, I ask them one question, "How do you want to solve that?" Niel asks, "What do you want me to do?"

Managers and leaders hate hearing people complain, which, when they come with no solution, that's what it is. People who bring only problems appear as whining, and that's not effective. Bring solutions to offer for discussion.

Share Information and Be Transparent

Make sure you hold nothing back from your non-collaborator. If you do and she finds out, she will never trust you again, making it difficult to collaborate. This might be difficult if your non-collaborator is not trustworthy or has broken your trust with her. Protect yourself, but not at the cost of withholding information that may cause your non-collaborator or you to fail.

Provide information as soon as you have it and post it so it will not be lost when it might be needed again. Many times non-collaborators withhold information at the beginning of the project and when the project starts to fail, they jump in and provide the information so that they can be seen as heroes by rescuing the project. And what does the organization do? Reward the hero! We thus reinforce the non-collaborative behavior.

Communication Delivery

Who delivers your communication and when are important. Include more than you and your non-collaborator in all conversations. Have someone else deliver the message. And if you or your collaborator are having a bad day, wait to give him your message.

Have Three People in the Collaboration

"Sam, you committed to having your report in by Friday. How is it going?"

"I never said I would finish by Friday!"

How many times have we heard something like this? People will say something in a one-on-one conversation and then deny that they ever said it. This makes it difficult to move forward and solve the issue or exploit the opportunity—you are too busy arguing about what you agreed to.

An effective way to avoid an argument like this is the "three people concept," which is based on game theory [3]. If there are only two people in the conversation and one withholds information, it is difficult for the other person to detect. If there are three people and one withholds information, the other two have a much better chance at detecting that information is being withheld. Always have a third person in the room when you have a conversation with a non-collaborator. This does not mean that the third person is in your corner. She can be neutral but she needs to be present.

Find an Influencer to Influence Your Non-Collaborator

I see it again and again: group decisions being filtered or altered by communication through the team leader only—providing a possibly unrealistic or an incorrect interpretation of what the team decides. One leader, Sally, was concerned with the decisions of a committee reported to her by the committee chair, always by phone and with just the two of them on the line. Because Sally knew all the people on the committee, she thought what the chair reported didn't sound like decisions they would make. When she checked with the committee members, they said they certainly had not agreed with the decisions the chair had reported. In her next call, Sally confronted the chair with what she had heard from the committee members. The chair denied it and repeated her original set of decisions.

This went on for six months. No matter how many times Sally asked, the chair always said, "That's what the committee wants." Finally, Sally reached out to someone the chair respected and would listen to. This influencer got the chairperson to see the value in what the committee wanted to do and report it correctly.

Watch Your Timing

If your non-collaborator is having a bad day, stand back. Wait for a better time to collaborate. One time a member of my team completely blew up a project iteration. The team dealt with the fallout and moved on. Two weeks later, that team member came to me and asked for a raise. That is bad timing.

Be sensitive to what else is going on the lives of your non-collaborators. Are they under pressure themselves? Are they working on a tight project deadline? Are they distracted? If so, give them some room and time and watch for the right opportunity to have a real, meaningful collaboration.

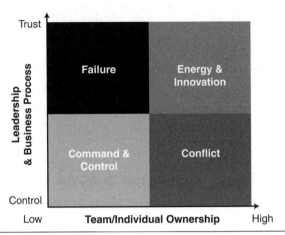

FIGURE 8.2   The Trust-Ownership Model

Specific Techniques for Dealing with Non-Collaborators

With the help of the Trust-Ownership Model, we can map the traits of non-collaborators to each of the quadrants in Figure 8.2. Based on those traits, we can then think of ways to move the non-collaborator toward Energy and Innovation. Remember that this is a spectrum and your non-collaborator could sit in more than one quadrant.

Where do we start? By answering the question, "Where is your non-collaborator on the model?"

Now, let's take a look at each quadrant.

Conflict

I was just going to bed when I noticed my dog, Missy, wanted to go out. My housemate said, "She's okay. She doesn't need to go out." It sure didn't look that way to me. If Missy were able to stand up, she would have been crossing her legs and doing an "I have to go" dance. So, I let her out. Of course, once she got outside, there were many more interesting things to do out there than just do her business. She refused to come back in the house. I was stuck. Here

I was, standing outside trying to get a recalcitrant dog to listen to her very forgiving master.

However, my housemate always could get Missy to obey her, but my housemate was already asleep. What to do, what to do? Having no other choice, I got her up. As you might expect, she was not too happy. When she finally came outside, she said, "Why did you let her outside?" My response? "That's not helping me get her to come inside." "But I told you not to let her out." And again, I replied, "That may be true, but that is not helping get Missy inside."

This is an example of Appreciative Inquiry (AI),[1] a tool to stay out of the blame game (because there is absolutely no value, zero, in blaming people or processes) and focus on how to move forward. The old form of problem solving is to identify the problem, analyze the causes, and plan the actions. The basic assumption is that there is a problem to be solved. AI values what exists, envisions what can be, and discusses the next steps. This assumes an organization and the people know about and want to focus on the future possibility.

Old ways of solving problems look back at what went wrong, what happened, who is to blame, and how we fix what went wrong. AI looks forward: what's working, what's possible, and how we can achieve it. We call this "falling forward" to remind ourselves that we learn more from how we recover from our mistakes than figuring out how we made the mistakes.

Often, non-collaborators don't want to participate because they don't believe in the solution. One way to engage such non-collaborators is to spend time, with at least three people in the room, brainstorming and discussing the pros and cons of various potential solutions.

When doing this, try to find something you can agree on—no matter how small. In one particularly tense situation, one person resisted collaborating, was uncooperative, and resistant to everything until I found she had a dog that she was fond of. Because I also love my dog, we found some common ground—completely unrelated to the topic of our conflict. With this dog-lover relationship, we had a starting point and things moved forward.

---

1. David Cooperrider is generally credited with coining the term "Appreciative Inquiry."

Micromanagement

Nothing, and we mean nothing, is worse than some-one telling you what to do, how to do it, and by when. People are not chess pieces. And when someone treats them like they are, they give up and do the minimum to get by. They don't feel trusted or valued.

What can we do about micromanagement? Under-stand why the non-collaborator micromanages. Is it fear of failure, fear of losing control? Is he afraid to be wrong? Using the Macro-Leadership Cube (see Chapter 5, Ownership Tools), build a cube together where the walls of the cube are results, budget, marketing window, resources, and so on. The results must be specific and measureable. Then ask the microman-ager to step back while you or the team's work remains inside the cube.

Sarah was going into a meeting with her micromanager boss. Tired of being judged by how she did her work rather than by the results of her work, she asked her boss if she had done something wrong. "No," he answered. "Well," she said, "that's the way I feel when you tell me in detail what I need to do. When you do that, I feel as if you don't trust me." He was surprised and said he didn't mean it that way and it never happened again.

Check in regularly so there are no worries about what you are doing.

The Passive Non-Collaborator

This type of non-collaboration could be due to fear, lack of understanding, cultural differences, and lack of interest in the goals. When dealing with passive non-collaborators, ask questions that attempt to develop some passion for the goals and results. Ask what they care about, what is holding them back from contribut-ing or pursuing their passion, and advocate for them to pursue their area of passion (even if it means they find that passion somewhere else).

The Passive-Aggressive Non-Collaborator

In general, this is a competitive person with a lack of respect for others. Such a person is often all about self-preservation or pursuing a personal agenda. Whatever you do, *do not* engage in a power struggle with this person because once you engage, she has won. Wrap her in the process and make her step into her responsibility by making it the only step she can take.

"What if we don't have a process to wrap them in?" someone asked.

"Make one up," was my answer. "Where do you think some processes come from?"

Make them commit in public, with at least two other people in the room. Take the fun out of being dysfunctional. If people are disruptive, look closely to see if they are getting a reward and remove it. Even negative feedback can be a reward for some people.

When they say, "That will never work," ask them how they would solve it. Again, make sure there are at least two other people listening. Whatever you do, don't let a passive-aggressive person be in a leadership position—his team is often the target of his aggression.

Non-Collaborating Processes

At dinner one night at a conference with a peer, we talked about performance reviews.

"I can't stay long, I have to do the performance reviews of my team."

"Why are you doing them?" I asked. "Didn't they set their own goals? "Yes."

"Then let them evaluate themselves and send it directly to your HR department. They know more about how well they have achieved their goals than you do."

Weeks later I saw my friend at another meeting and asked how it went. "I did what you suggested, and it was great." And her team agreed.

No doubt about it, independent performance reviews, especially those with stack ranking, will be the most difficult to overcome. Explain the Trust-Ownership Model to your HR department and ask them to take ownership of helping set up evaluations that help teams collaborate to reach the Energy and Innovation state. Ask "why" they do independent performance reviews, and explain their detriment to team collaboration. And bring data! Check out Alfie Kohn's book, *Punished by Rewards* [3]. Start with Chapter 10, page 181.

Some years ago I was running the education department of a local university and one of the administrators came to see me.

"Don't be cross, but I've done something against the rules," she said. "One of our students was looking for a computer-based language training book, but all the ones we have are loaned out, so I just went to the local store and bought one without approval. It would have taken ages to get the spending approved and she needed it right away."

Far from being upset, I was delighted. I publically gave her recognition in front of the whole team and I personally handled the escalation with the procurement process.

Whatever you do, don't let a process cause you to fail.

Team-to-Team Collaboration

Whatever we say, no matter how much we would like to avoid dependencies in our work, we have to collaborate with other teams. And it is not always easy. First, each team may have their own priorities, especially if the two teams have different bosses. Sure, eventually, if you go up the food chain, we all have the same boss. But, who has the time or the credibility to not take care of things at our level?

In many cases, there is tension between marketing and engineering—two teams that should and must work together but have very different styles and goals. They rarely act as one team. They seem to see each other as the enemy.

The marketing viewpoint? "They don't deliver." "They take too long." "Who knows what I'll get and when?" "They make things too complicated." "The customers aren't happy. There are too many issues in the field." "They have to do what they are told and they don't."

And engineering's perspective on marketing? "They keep changing the priorities." "They think it's simple to build." "They don't really know what the customers want." "We don't get good direction." "Our questions are not answered fast enough." "They don't understand technology."

One way to set up such teams for success is the Product/Project Inception Planning tool we describe in Chapter 6, Business Alignment Tools. When the teams come together and collaborate with a common goal in mind, they agree as to priorities, risks, and opportunities to reduce complexity and uncertainty.

Remember, it is really *one* team. Refer to it as a "whole team" or "megateam." Don't quantify it by using "our team" and "your team." It's one team.

One of the important elements of this inception process is to build a common vision together. Use a sticky note exercise to brainstorm the product potential and the critical success factors. Openly discuss what everyone sees and find one vision together. As described in Chapter 6, use this vision to define decision filters the team will use to hold to the vision. Remember and use the vision and the decision filters at each meeting.

Validate each other. Discuss why you need the skills and abilities from each team to reach the vision and goal. Accept risks collectively. Risks are the whole team's risks.

And hold past dodgers accountable. At the end of every action generating meeting, ask everyone, "How are we going to hold each other accountable?"

Working Around Your Non-Collaborator

Suppose you have tried all of these tools and your non-collaborator will still not collaborate with you. First, when you encounter him, reflect, don't react. You don't have to respond to a question from him right away. Take a minute. One of my favorite responses in such a situation is, "I'll get back to you on that." It gives me some time to process how I want to respond to my non-collaborator. And don't take it personally. Don't react if he has pressed one of your "hot buttons." And if you can't remain calm, leave the room.

If you are the leader and need to have the non-collaborator off the team but you can't make that happen, sideline him. Make sure he has no critical path tasks or any task the rest of the team depends on. The team will instantly know what you have done. If you don't deal with the disruptive non-collaborator, the team will be angry with you because they are carrying the burden of this obstructionist.

Whatever happens, make sure you protect your team.

What if your non-collaborator is your boss? Some techniques are included in the section, Managing Up. However, it may be time to move on to another position within the company—or to another company.

In Summary

It is much more important to generate value and reduce time to value than it is to hit a date. Ideally, we do all three. But if we must sacrifice anything, let the date move and focus intently on delivering value. Value comes when we innovate in what creates our unique value proposition and standardize around best practices for everything else. And remember, it is our customer who defines value.

When a manager begins interfering with the team's focus and creates unnecessary distractions, productivity decreases. A leader, either of the team or in the team, can manage this manager using several techniques: providing the data and reports himself; using the Macro-Leadership Cube to help the manager understand the boundaries of the team efforts and let them work inside that cube; show progress and check in often. Work on keeping the manager from disrupting the team's progress.

Collaborating is essential to the delivery of value to customers. However, there may be people who don't want to collaborate. In this section, we talked about the steps and tools to try to collaborate with this resistance.

- Identify why your non-collaborators do not want to collaborate.
- Understand the system they work in, what motivates them, how they are acknowledged, how they define success, and so on.
- Understand the system you work in and the level of risk you are willing to take on.
- Use specific and general techniques to collaborate with your non-collaborators.

References

[1] Bennis, Warren. *Beyond Bureaucracy: Essays on the Development and Evolution of Human Organization*. San Francisco: Jossey-Bass, 1993.

[2] Nash, John. "Two-Person Cooperative Games." *Econometrica*. Vol. 21, No. 1 (Jan., 1953), pp. 128–140.

[3] Kohn, Alfie. *Punished by Rewards: The Trouble with Gold Stars, Incentive Plans, A's, Praise, and Other Bribes*. 2nd Edition. Mariner Books, 1999.

CHAPTER 9

METRICS

The Big Ideas

- People do what they are measured by.
- We need metrics that focus on delivering business value, foster trust, and do not take away ownership.
- If we are moving toward Energy and Innovation (the green) we need an indication of the progress we are making so that we can tune our actions.

Why Metrics Matter

I have spent my career consumed by metrics. According to the old saw, "If you can measure it, you can manage it." In our quest to manage everything, we sometimes implement a wide range of overlapping, competing metrics and sometimes useless ones. For example, a few years ago a technology company asked me to work with its software engineering team to finalize how to effectively measure software productivity and quality. My first interaction with the team was to review the metrics they had already defined and agreed were important. The head of engineering proudly fired up the projector so that he could show me on the big screen the 63 metrics the department had decided were critical.

I was taken aback. "Sixty-three? Do you think that covers it all or are you missing some?"

The head of engineering was not yet used to my cynical observations and so replied, "Well, there are some others that we could not get consensus on that some felt were important. They are on a different worksheet."

163

He then highlighted a different tab to show the 19 other metrics that could have made the cut, and continued, "If you think these are worth including, I am sure we can figure out a way to get them in."

I looked around the room. This group had put a lot of effort into defining these measures, and I did not want to devalue their work in any way, but 63 metrics? My personal rule of thumb is that you need only five to seven metrics. Any more than that and you are likely trending into meaningless measures. But how could I get that point across without causing harm?

Then, I had an epiphany. "We want metrics that help us discriminate between activity and accomplishment. With good metrics, we will know that we are getting things done, not just being busy. Let's take a look at your metrics. Which align with getting the right things done, making progress on your critical business goals?"

With this, we launched into a great conversation about meaningful metrics. We ended up with seven measures that met my guidelines. The agreed-upon metrics

- Were focused on measuring progress toward business goals—thus meeting the accomplishment-over-activity criterion.
- Were few in number—otherwise the sheer volume makes them meaningless.
- Motivated the right behaviors rather than being something used as a weapon against others. Too often we impose metrics to punish wrong behaviors rather than inspire improved performance.
- Were designed to measure processes, not people. Meaningful metrics help us identify when processes, not people, need to be fixed.
- Were simple to measure and simple to understand.

Good metrics are essential in enabling and encouraging fact-based action in business and can have a powerful effect in helping teams focus on business value and collaboration.

However, we have all seen many cases where ill-considered, bad metrics have caused counterproductive motivation and severe damage:

- Mortgage salesmen who were measured and rewarded on sales rather than long-term profitability and sustainability are at the root of much of today's world financial crisis.
- Programmers measured on schedule rather than business value create poorly targeted code with low quality, which is costly to maintain and decreases revenues.

- Support center operatives are measured on number of calls handled or call length rather than customer satisfaction. The consequence is abrupt termination of calls, resulting in increasing numbers of calls, unhappy customers, and loss of business.
- Salesmen measured on individual product sales sell inappropriate solutions that don't perform, damaging both the customers' and the business's reputation.

When Lou Gerstner took over as CEO of IBM, the company was tearing itself apart because of internal competition. At that time, business unit success (and executive reward) was measured independently for each division with the *intent* of motivating teams to deliver increasing value. A nasty side effect was that business units were effectively in competition for, and often in front of, the customer and not motivated to help each other deliver the best end-to-end, totally integrated solutions. Gerstner was told by many that he needed to change the metrics in order to rebuild an IBM-wide focus on customer success. Lou's immediate response was that individuals needed to ignore the current dysfunctional metrics and collaborate to do what they knew to be right for the customer and for the business. Over the next several years measurements and reward schemes were modified to cover larger organizational elements until they were eventually based on the whole of IBM's performance. This not only removed the motivation for competition with internal teams and individuals, but also sent a strong signal that collaboration to deliver business value to the customer was the highest priority.

Bad metrics can create boundaries, suboptimization, and conflict, all of which result in poor performance and lost revenue. Good metrics, which focus on overall customer and business value, naturally foster collaboration and ownership. So what are the good metrics? In this chapter, we explore what metrics will maximize the delivery of business value, support dealing honestly with ambiguity, foster trust and collaboration, and not take away ownership.

Integrity

Before we get into a discussion about metrics we must start with the overall environment in which they are used.

The foundational requirement of good metrics is, yet again, integrity and honesty.

- Plans must be honestly acknowledged as a goal, the most likely outcome, and not as an inflexible straightjacket.
- Accuracy must not be expected or claimed where it does not or cannot exist. Effort estimates are just that, estimates with a significant degree of uncertainty.
- Actions and owners must be focused correctly. For example, productivity measures are often used with the intent of motivating individuals to deliver more, rather than as a measure for the leader or executive who *really* has the responsibility to enable and support the team.
- Care must always be taken to ensure that the common problems such as gaming the system and green shift (the tendency of the outlook and status to get better as they are reported higher up the organization) are countered effectively. Try to make the measures completely objective, and where that is not possible, consider how those asked to provide the data will feel and act, especially if they believe that the data will reflect on their performance.

Overall metrics must be seen to be honest and allow for honesty. Failure here will drive a huge wedge between the delivery teams and the business.

Development teams are often measured on the number of problems arising from the product's use in customer environments. With one team, management wanted detailed explanations of minor variations in the number of customer problem reports, wasting large amounts of the leader's and team's effort. When the team tried to explain that this was statistical noise, they were overruled and told they were being unhelpful. The team soon learned that the executives involved were mathematically incompetent and more focused on demonstrating their own power than really improving customer experience. Pay attention to statistics. When numbers are small, variations are often statistical noise.

Note that even without integrity in the measurements, good individuals and teams will often still do what is correct for the customer and the business even if the measure drives them in the opposite direction. While this behavior can mitigate the problem, it still generates a feeling within the team that management is incompetent and untrustworthy. It is also difficult for individuals to sustain this position, and if management does not change, the team will eventually give up and conform to the bad measures.

Even well-intentioned teams will be worn down by poorly targeted metrics.

Results Not Process

On the electronic stock exchange project, the team was building a workstation for the traders. Remember, the traders were trading on the floor so we had no workstation to look at. The team built the first user interface prototype and set out to the first meeting with some traders.

"How did it go?" their manager asked.

"Don't worry. We will reuse some of that code."

"I don't care," was the reply. "I only care about one thing. When the system goes live, no trader throws a workstation out the window."

After 20 years, no workstation has ever been thrown out the window.

The key measure here was customer acceptance and not internal development metrics.

Many project failures arise from measuring the process rather than the result or the outcomes. Take for example, following the plan, the worst measure you can make. Why? What if we learn the customer doesn't want something? What if the customer wants something different? What if we miss something the business needs? The team may meet the date but it may have poor quality. Ownership is taken away from the teams and falls to the process.

Teams are essentially being told to "follow the process" rather than focusing on meeting customer and business needs. These types of measures disconnect the team from the business and customer and can result in products that no one wants or one that customers hate to use.

Process-based measures are always subject to gaming—getting around the measurement. If development effectiveness is measured by the amount of code delivered to test, you can be sure that the code quality will be poor and the overall defects and costs will rise. Much better to measure unit test escapes, which have a very significant effect on overall productivity. (A defect missed in unit test but found later will cost very much more development effort to diagnose and fix.) If process based metrics cannot be avoided then honestly consider how they will be gamed and what mitigations you can put in place. The more controlling the process is, the more it gets in the way of the team doing the right thing, the more it will be gamed.

The most effective measures are strongly aligned to outcomes such as business and customer results. No amount of internal measures can disguise actual customer satisfaction or real business results. Results or outcome-based measures cannot be gamed.

Whatever you do, make sure your metrics do not remove ownership from the delivery team in any way.

Learning Not Punishment

Someone once said it is only a failure if you don't learn from it.

When metrics are used to place blame, individuals and teams will always present information in a positive light to avoid getting blamed. In this case the chance for making any needed improvement is lost and everyone is encouraged to game the system.

Base your metrics on learning. Every problem is an opportunity for improvement. Every failure is an opportunity to learn a better solution. Any new innovation and product can come from learning what customers really want, what will delight them.

If teams or individuals believe that the metrics will be used against them, you can be sure the data will be adjusted to make them look good in the eyes of the business.

If metrics are used for a purpose other than learning (often as some form of competitive comparison between teams) they will be gamed. Gaming this type of measurement system occurs all the time, even if the metrics are well chosen. If you must take this approach, make data input automatic if possible but otherwise as easy as possible without sacrificing data quality. Explain to teams that you are well aware of the possibility of gaming. Show them how gaming the metrics actually hurts the learning process and the business.

Some years ago, a company was trying to assess the deployment of specific agile iterative practices. Initially each team was polled and asked whether the practices were used. Results were generally seen to be good. Sometime later, as part of a wider assessment of Agile credibility and adoption, an anonymous survey was carried out, polling individuals across the company. Results were aggregated only at a major organizational level. With the fear of identification (and potential punishment) removed, the results were markedly different and very much lower. These indicated that much more action was needed to educate and promote the use of agile practices throughout the organization, while the "official" statistics were saying that all was well.

Measuring Culture Change

While metrics, in general, have a strong effect on culture, we will first focus on ways of assessing our progress in *building* an effective culture. We cover metrics in general in the next section. Here we are looking specifically at assessing the state of our organization, its leadership and culture.

As leaders work to change the culture within their organization they urgently need feedback on the progress they are making. And they need early indications to know when and how to modify their course.

How can we measure that we are successfully moving into the green? By measuring

- Leadership effectiveness in enabling the change
- Trust
- Ownership
- Business alignment and purpose
- Honestly dealing with ambiguity and complexity

Let's take a closer look.

Measurements

Measuring cultural change is difficult. We have identified the areas that we need to assess, but these are far from simple metrics. You will need a good degree of judgment. In the sections that follow we will identify simple metrics where possible. Where these are not available, we will identify a set of questions you can ask yourself that will give you positive and negative indicators of progress.

A common approach is to survey the workers within the organization and ask them to anonymously rate their environment for the five characteristics we've listed here. If it makes sense in your organization, we recommend the use of the Net Promoter Score (NPS) for this. This may not give an accurate overall view of the situation, but it will certainly give the working-level view.

The Net Promoter Score is a common industry approach developed by Fred Reichheld[1] and explained in a *Harvard Business Review* article [1]. Full explanations and the rationale of the approach are easily found on the web, but essentially you ask the "customers" of a product or service how likely they would be—on a scale of 1 to 10—to recommend your products and services to their peers, friends, families, et cetera. Those who score the service 9 or 10 are considered "promoters" (they like your product/service). Those who score the service 1 to 6 are considered "detractors" (they don't like your product/service), and those who score 7 or 8 are neutral. The NPS is calculated as the percentage of promoters less the percentage of detractors. This means that the NPS can run from +100% where everyone recommends your product or service to −100% where everyone thinks it valueless.

Another method to measure your progress is to run a collaborative sticky note session with the team. (See Appendix C, Collaboration Process.) In this session ask them what would make them more effective. This is the approach we used to gather the information presented in the introduction to the Trust-Ownership Model. Its power is that it will give a strong indication of the areas that need work without biasing the response by asking questions about specific areas of leadership behavior, business processes, or anything else. If improving trust comes at the top of your list, then that is what you most need to work on.

Leadership Effectiveness Metrics

The most critical factor in building a powerful culture is the effectiveness of our leaders. And the most useful measure of leadership effectiveness in promoting a new culture or approach is the leader's Net Promoter Score (NPS). When we ask teams how much value there is in a new approach (i.e., would they recommend their leader's approach to their peers?) we get insight into our progress in building an understanding of the value of the approach. As with any survey-style metrics, it is important to set up the survey so that individuals do not feel in any way pressured to affirm progress. The usual way to do this is to make the survey anonymous and publish data only at an aggregate level.

---

1. http://www.netpromotersystem.com/about/index.aspx

As IBM worked to promote the use of Agile across the company, it measured its progress on both mindset and deployment. The first measurement was an NPS on the agile practices being used. We set up a survey so that individuals could provide their opinions of the value of agile practices within their organization. One of the questions was, "On a scale of 1 to 10, would you recommend the use of short iterations to your peers?" We calculated the NPS from the results and used the scores to assess our progress in explaining the value of the practices to the development teams. A strong positive score indicated that teams valued and were likely to use the practice without further encouragement. Low scores indicated that the practice was not seen as having value to the team and showed us that we had more work to do.

We were initially concerned that there might be a bias—those who were passionate about Agile would vote while others would opt out of the survey. However, the resulting data showed a nice distribution of both positive and negative scores across the practices, suggesting that this was not a significant issue.

The cycle between survey and action was very short. Simply sharing the results with the owners of the major divisions immediately allowed them to take action to increase support and training where needed. The only practical limitation was survey fatigue, and so we decided to conduct the survey only once each year.

Even better, it cost almost nothing to conduct this survey. It was a single web page that could be completed quickly.

If you are organizing and conducting a survey, make it as attractive and as easy as possible. Resist the natural tendency to create a comprehensive, complex survey. The longer the survey takes to complete, the lower the participation and the harder to collect and synthesize the results.

In addition to identifying action areas, simply carrying out a survey demonstrates that leaders are engaged. Good leadership effectiveness metric examples include the following:

- NPS surveys on practices. Are the new practices well regarded? Are they adding value?
- Wider organizational acceptance of the new approach. How well do the business processes support the new practices?

As we rolled out new practices in several companies, we polled the development teams on the degree to which the organizational infrastructure, such as the business processes, finance, audit, IT, and legal, supported the new practices. We rated them on a simple 1-to-5 scale:

1. Requires the new approach.
2. Encourages the new approach.
3. Is neutral.
4. Makes the new approach difficult.
5. Prohibits the new approach.

This allowed us to work with the infrastructure areas to ensure that they were fully enabling the overall business initiative.

Bad leadership effectiveness metric examples include publicly asking teams and individuals if they are using the new methods. This almost always leads to gaming, as teams report what they believe management wants to hear.

Trust

How much trust does the leadership have in the professional teams? How do the teams see this trust? Do they believe that they are trusted?

This is difficult to assess. Great Place to Work[2] uses a complex survey, but most of us need simpler measures.

As mentioned earlier, our approach of asking teams what would make them more productive and then looking to see where "increasing trust" appears in the list gives a good idea of what the team believes it needs.

Other alternatives you can use to assess the *team's* view include asking the team members

- Do you feel trusted (Yes or No or Some of the Time)
- Do you trust your team members?
- Do you trust the organization?
- Do you trust the organization's processes?

---

2. http://www.greatplacetowork.com

Here are some questions you can use to assess *your* trust (and the organization's trust) in your teams:

- What do you trust your teams to own?
- What do you have to approve before teams can act?
- To what extent do your teams decide what to deliver and by when, based on their own assessments rather than being told?
- Do the teams feel that they can make decisions about what will be delivered and by when?
- Do they track and manage their own progress?
- Are your teams able to make significant decisions without separate management review, or are all decisions made by management?
- Is trust trending up or down?

Ownership

It is also challenging to assess the degree to which teams feel that they have ownership of the business commitments. You can do it best by looking at the behaviors of the teams.

- Do your teams make their own commitments?
- Do they meet their commitments?
- Do they track and manage their own progress?
- Do they have sufficient information to make those decisions in line with business needs?
- Do they understand the business pressures and the needs of the business?
- Do they understand the unique value proposition of their project?
- Do they understand the business goals?
- How well can they map their projects to these goals?

Dealing Honestly with Ambiguity

This is one of the most important and yet challenging measures, particularly because of our personal and organizational quest for certainty.

The easiest way to get the team's view of this is to ask them using a version of the NPS: On a scale of 1 to 10, how well do you feel we deal *honestly* with ambiguity?

And there are some obvious questions you can ask yourself:

- Do the business templates include assessments of the uncertainty in any estimate? How do you use these?
- Do you make commitments without involving those charged with implementation?
- Do your plans admit to no modification?
- Is your primary measure of good governance how well people conform to a plan?

The Trust-Ownership Assessment in Chapter 3, Building Trust and Ownership, and Appendix B, Trust-Ownership Assessment, also provide a template for assessing your progress toward Energy and Innovation. Assess your progress often and look for trends.

Metrics Walls

In the introduction to this chapter, we gave a number of examples of the types of metrics that can compromise the effective delivery of business value by

- Focusing on process rather than results.
- Building competition between teams or team members.
- Encouraging a short-term view.
- Wasting time collecting and reporting ineffective metrics.
- Encouraging leaders to build a command and control approach by reviewing detailed (and perhaps meaningless) metrics on a regular basis.

Bad metrics can be a wall that stands between your team and Energy and Innovation. In this section, we introduce a set of guidelines that you can use to evaluate your metrics and identify any that are getting in the way of trust and ownership. You can then eliminate or replace the metrics.

Having too many, and often conflicting, metrics disempowers the team and distracts it from working on actual delivery.

Let's look at a couple of examples.

On taking over a pretty effective team that was using an iterative development process, one of our favorite directors, Nickie, asked that the team stop creating and sending her status reports. She told the team that there was no need to create any reports that they themselves did not consider useful. If she wanted detailed status she said she would listen in on the daily team meeting or have a look at the team's dashboard. For tracking processes she would attend each iteration reflection to join in the discussion on what had been achieved compared to their goals, the overall project outlook, and the improvement actions being taken.

She made it very clear that the responsibility for delivery was theirs and that she needed to be consulted only if they needed help from her. This immediately showed an increased level of trust. She would rely on the metrics *they* were using to measure their progress rather than burden them with her own.

Another leader, at risk of having his team's time wasted by a more senior executive and inveterate micromanager, protected his team by taking over the responsibility of collecting the data and presenting it to the micromanager. His view was that there was no way that he was wasting his team's time creating metrics that they didn't value.

Are Our Metrics of Any Use?

How do we make sure that the metrics we are using are effective and not just vehicles for giving leaders a feeling of power and control while not achieving anything useful? How do we know the metrics we want to create will be of any value?

Let's look at some general rules of thumb for metrics:

- **The fewer metrics, the better.** Choose those that will have the most significant impact. When these have made good progress, consider changing the metric in an iterative way
- **Minimize negative side effects.** Remember that all metrics have strong side effects and that you must be aware of the potential negative impacts of optimizing for a specific goal. Select metrics that complement each other or counterbalance each other. For example, you can measure expense reduction to increase profit margins, but you run the risk of increasing time-to-market or decreasing quality.
- **People do what they are measured by.** The underlying truth is that people's behavior is always shaped by how they believe they are measured. Meaningful metrics result in meaningful and productive behavior changes. Meaningless metrics result in meaningless and counterproductive behavior changes.

Getting Useful Metrics, Removing the Rest

How can we tell useful metrics from damaging ones? In this section, we will look at whether your current metrics or any new ones you want to create are truly effective. We need to consider

- What is your goal; what you are trying to achieve?
- Is the metric valuable to the team that is using it?
- How long will it remain valuable?
- What is the cycle time for action based on this measure?
- Are the candidate measures actually aligned with the business needs?
- Do they build ownership with the team?
- What is the true cost of collecting and analyzing the data?
- What are the side effects of using this measure?
- How could they be misused and damage our focus on value delivery?

Let's look at each of these in more detail.

What Are We Trying to Achieve?

Before selecting any metrics, first consider what it is that you want to achieve, what decisions you need to make, and questions you need to answer. Use these goals to help you select the appropriate metrics. Never measure things just because you can.

This is a fundamental starting point. There are many metrics that we can collect and report but that are a distraction from where the focus should be. Many of these are labeled "vanity metrics," a term coined by Eric Ries in his book, *The Lean Startup* [2]. Vanity metrics are metrics that are not actionable. As a simple rule of thumb you should beware of vanity metrics.

Businesses need to focus. Large numbers of metrics cause loss of focus and paralysis among leaders. Start by deciding what your most important issues are, and then create metrics to help you improve in these areas. As each improves to an acceptable level, choose a new area for improvement and iterate.

Some years ago, a software development team was suffering from growing technical debt.[3] As the debt grew, it became more difficult to assemble the product. Testing time was extended and quality still suffered. The leaders felt that business pressures to meet a commitment schedule were causing the teams to cut corners in unit testing. Because meeting the schedule was their primary measure of success, the quality was deteriorating as teams rushed through the unit testing process.

To test their theory about the suspected cause and effect relationship, the leaders started measuring how much of the code submitted to the library was covered by automated testing scripts. They captured the data and, without announcing anything specific to the teams, started displaying the results on a wall that was visible to the entire team. Over the next three months—and without ever formally announcing an initiative to improve automated test coverage—unit test coverage increased dramatically and the problems with product integration evaporated.

It is interesting to recognize that the team members obviously knew that they were cutting corners but, until the metrics made their compromises visible, their motivation to deliver on schedule was stronger than their motivation to deliver validated quality. By creating and publishing the measure, the leaders clearly demonstrated that they valued validated quality and the team modified its behavior accordingly. The leaders wanted to achieve improved quality and they found a metric to hit that goal.

Is the Metric Useful to the Team?

Metrics are most powerful when the teams choose those that will benefit them the most. (Imagine the trust that this requires from the teams' leaders!) Ask the team what measures would best help them achieve their goals. This not only increases the team's ownership of the process but also prevents the selection of inappropriate metrics. You can also ask if there are any current metrics that are getting in their way and are walls to reaching their goals?

---

3. Technical debt is anything that makes it difficult for the team to add value. It includes untested code, unfixed errors, and open design issues.

How Long Will the Metric Remain Useful?

Decide up front to avoid accumulating out-of-date metrics. Don't keep using metrics that are no longer useful. Once the metric has served its purpose and you have achieved the goal, consider dropping the metric unless it is, over the long term, motivational. After we've solved the problem we shouldn't need this measure until the end of time.

One team was having problems with code stability. During a retrospective they discovered no one was checking in code until the very *end* of the iteration, which did not allow for enough time to test. After some conversation, they decided to measure the number of check-ins per day. Over time, the team got into the habit of checking the code in several times a week. The code was then integrated and tested more frequently. As the code became more stable, they stopped measuring check-ins.

What Is the Cycle Time for Action?

Use the cycle time of the metrics to evaluate the effectiveness of the measure. The shorter the cycle the better. The sooner the team can get and incorporate feedback the better. Vanity metrics often have an infinite cycle time.

The two examples earlier are great examples of short cycle times. The check-in and code coverage measures were available daily, allowing the teams to respond immediately.

As an example of long-cycle-time metrics, think of waterfall processes with their end-of-project data analysis and review. Only at the end of the project does the team gather and assess feedback—way too late to make any impact on the project. Problems and actions the team identifies can, at best, only be implemented in the next full development cycle. Contrast this with the automated test code coverage example earlier. In this case the action cycle time was a single day. Results were gathered and published every night. Improvements were immediately visible.

Are the Candidate Measures Actually Aligned with the Business Needs?

Are the metrics fully aligned with increasing business value and collaboration? It is essential to honestly assess whether improvements in the metric will actually lead to the delivery of increased business value.

An organization we worked with used a typical Stage-Gate process for product development. They assessed product quality just prior to product launch. The company found that it was having difficult discussions about how many of the known remaining defects they should let loose on their customers. Perhaps a valuable metric to measure their product development process would be how often they completed a cycle without any known defects. This would align with a goal of avoiding the delivery of any known defects to their customers (which never seemed to make the customers happy or satisfied with their products)—a much better measure of customer value.

In teams using iterative methods, a common predictive measure is the technical debt in *each* iteration. A team using iterative methods for the first time focused on keeping this measure as low as possible. Their goal was to complete as many iterations as possible without any serious open defects. As the project neared completion, the normally difficult questions about whether or not the product was good enough to launch went away and they dramatically reduced the number of defects occurring at the customer site.

Do the Measures Reinforce Ownership in the Team or Remove It?

These metrics are similar to those for alignment. Do the metrics allow the team freedom to define and take the actions that they think are strongly aligned with the delivery of business value?

One company we worked with measured aggregate customer field problems from its shipped products. The numbers of problems each month rose and fell in a random way but the overall trend was generally favorable as the team improved its processes. Unfortunately, the executive responsible for the customer support team, in monthly review meetings, used the statistical noise in the data as a stick to berate the product teams—even though there were no sensible short-term actions the teams could take. The result was that everyone but the executive in charge felt these meeting were a complete waste of time. The product teams felt no ownership for the data or the actions forced upon them. In fact, the process devalued the focus on the customer experience.

In parallel with this useless activity (and unknown to the executive), the product teams spent time looking for and getting to the root causes on what created the problems. They then attacked these and measured those results. This measure, as compared to the meaningless metric, was highly useful to the teams and reinforced their ownership of product quality and the customer experience. Focusing on this metric delivered an ongoing improvement trend that was largely ignored by the customer support executive.

What Is the True Cost of Collecting and Analyzing the Data?

Always ensure that the cost of collecting the metric is significantly less than the value that it can deliver. And we do mean significantly less.

Recognize that the cost of collecting data is not zero and can sometimes be very high, especially if it involves continuous action by the delivery team members. This cost is often ignored and can have a huge negative impact on team productivity.

Some time ago, I was asked by a senior executive to analyze the amount of code and architecture reuse across our organization. We had a fairly good idea of the amount of reuse but I estimated that it would take more than 20 person-years to just collect the provenance of each piece of code in our libraries! So what was I going to do? Consume 20+ person-years of resource to collect incredibly detailed reuse data? Rather than do that, I personally did some sample analysis and validated this with a selection of seasoned professionals. I then returned to the senior executive and gave my report based on this high-level approach.

"Well, how much reuse do we have?" the executive asked.

"Quite a bit," was my answer. "But it varies greatly between different environments."

"Hmmm," was his reply, "that's what I expected."

This high-level estimate was sufficient for the executive's purpose and didn't require costly gathering of detailed data.

As the data collection can be expensive, so can the analysis. We once ran a survey that generated over 6,000 write-in comments. Imagine the time to read, categorize, and analyze this unstructured data.

Remember to especially look for direct impacts on the development team. One team we worked with was doing a detailed "causal" analysis and categorization of *every* defect that they fixed in *development*. This involved answering 20 or so difficult questions about the root cause and characteristics of the defect. (Is this your definition of *useful*?) To ensure that this was done, the problem management system would not allow the defect to be closed until all the questions had been answered. The goal of this exercise was to give insight into weaknesses in the product, but it was totally ineffective. The time and cost to the individual developers were so high that many admitted to randomly selecting causes and characteristics (gaming the metric). In fact, the items at the top of the list of causes were the ones most often chosen (it took less effort to select from the top than to scroll down the list). It soon became obvious that this was a meaningless and expensive metric and the team decided they could provide more useful insight much more easily with a brief discussion between the developers as part of their retrospectives.

What Are the Side Effects of Using This Measure?

Look out for negative or unexpected side effects. Consider not only the intended goals but also how teams and individuals are likely to respond in both the short and the long term.

Leaders often evaluate the effectiveness of testing by the number of defects found by a set of independent testers. In this situation, testers are actually *rewarded* when they are given poor-quality product to test. They can then generate a large number of "found" defects that have the same underlying cause. By finding a large number of defects, they prove their value!

And why do the leaders use this metric? In theory, to motivate the testers to do more effective testing, which should lead to higher quality. And what is the result in real life? Measuring test teams this way is guaranteed to generate a highly confrontational relationship with the development team. After all, the development team is measured on zero defects. Thus begins the game. Was what the tester just classified as a defect really a defect or an artifact from an earlier version? What are the results of this confrontational relationship—confrontation driven by the side effects of metrics? Poor overall productivity, very low levels of morale, lower quality, and poor business value delivered.

In a real case, the leaders recognized this negative spiral and completely changed their approach. They abandoned this measure and brought the development and test teams together to enable effective collaboration to deliver quality. In this new arrangement, the testers sit next to and work with individual developers—even during unit test phases—and communicate face-to-face. The new metrics measure the growth in testing successes rather than defects found. Morale is higher and the whole team is working together to deliver increased business value.

Carefully consider the scope of a metric to ensure that it does not create suboptimal behavior.

How Could Metrics Be Misused and Damage Our Focus on Value Delivery?

With all metrics there is a potential for misuse. Sadly, management often pressures individuals to "enhance" data if they think the managers will be judged by the data. Deal with this up front, ideally by collecting data automatically from operational systems.

Many teams use velocity measures to assess and project progress. We recently worked with a team that was resizing their delivered stories after each iteration. We pointed out that this required significant work that did not add any value. After all, because they were adjusting both the delivered value and goal at each iteration, how could they assess their progress and improvement? In this situation, actual unadjusted velocity was a much better measure of their progress. The team agreed with us but told us that their management was misusing the measurement by rewarding or punishing them based on delivered velocity. To meet their velocity target, the team resized everything once they were done with their work. That way, their delivery velocity was always exactly on target—making the whole measure pointless.

Take a look at all the metrics in your organization that affect your team. Are they providing value or just getting in their way? Are there any metrics that would be useful to your team? If so, do they pass all the criteria described in the preceding sections?

The most damaging effect of metrics that add no value is that the team feels they are not trusted (they must be monitored on useless principles and waste time generating the data to show they are "effective") and they don't have ownership. Metrics, unfortunately, are easy to get wrong. And that comes with a high price tag for your organization, your teams, and your customers.

Metrics Programs

Please read the following at your peril. Many organizations feel that processes and metrics should be controlled and optimized by a central group. Such an approach removes ownership of process effectiveness, and the associated metrics to enable this, away from the delivery teams.

We do not like "metrics programs" and do not recommend them to anyone. Metrics programs can be a significant wall to trust and ownership.

But if you are being forced to implement a metrics program, here are some things to avoid. If you test the concepts of a metrics program against the criteria you have read in this chapter, you will see that such programs fail the "meaningful metrics" test in various ways.

Why Do Metrics Programs Fail?

Many metrics programs fail and many more do not achieve their intended goals. There are many reasons for this but some of the most common are

- Unclear goals and vision of what the organization is trying to achieve.
- Misuse of metrics for competitive comparisons or as a punishment rather than a learning process.
- Using metrics for political or other purposes rather than using them to help people to do their jobs more effectively and to deliver more value.
- Poor communication of the goals and intentions of the program to those involved.
- Focusing on process and not results.
- Too many metrics leading to lack of focus and ineffectiveness.
- Measuring vanity metrics.
- Measurements are not timely or the action cycle time is too long.
- Poor leadership, which is focused on the metrics process rather than its goals and effect.
- Not adapting to the changing needs of the business. Metrics will change over time and you need a mechanism to ensure they remain relevant and effective.

If you must have an organizational metrics program, then focus on using it to help individuals and teams learn how to take ownership of their own processes and the metrics for improving them. Focus on results-oriented rather than in-process metrics and work to help, support, and shield your teams.

Getting Started

We are often asked for a step-by-step guide, so here is a simple process.

1. Define the goals of your metrics.
   - Ensure the goals are fully aligned with the business.
   - Focus on learning rather than politics.
   - Enable action at the lowest level possible.
2. Involve the key players in deciding which specific metrics are going to be the most effective. Make sure you include those who are expected to take action.
3. Select the metrics you will use and how you will use them using the metric selection process we described earlier.
4. Communicate the metrics and goals of the metrics to all the teams. Explain why the metrics were chosen and how they will be used.
5. Regularly review the effectiveness of the metrics and be ready to change them regularly.

In Summary

As we work to improve the trust and ownership in our organization, we need clear indicators of progress so that we can focus our activities for best results.

The most valuable metric you can use is the team's view of the progress you are making.

- Are you, as a leader, effectively supporting and enabling the move to improved trust and ownership?
- Does the team feel trusted enough to take effective action without asking for permission or approval?
- Is the team able and willing to take ownership of their deliveries?

- Is the team purpose aligned with the business goals?
- Does the organization deal honestly with ambiguity?

Using these metrics will enable you to focus on the most effective actions to take to move forward.

Using metrics effectively is much more difficult than it appears to be. Badly chosen metrics can mislead and drive counterproductive behaviors. However, well-chosen metrics can be a powerful enabler and motivator of effective action.

References

[1] Reichheld, Frederick F. "The One Number You Need to Grow." *Harvard Business Review*. December 2003.

[2] Ries, Eric. *The Lean Startup: How Today's Entrepreneurs Use Continuous Innovation to Create Radically Successful Businesses*. Crown Business, 2011.

CHAPTER 10

CASE STUDY

Sometimes you just cannot quite fathom what you signed up for. The interviewing process had lasted a couple of months. This process was something of a joint "tire-kicking." They did a lot of due diligence on me and I thought I had done a lot of due diligence on them. They had been very clear about the limited role they wanted me, their new CIO, to play.

This e-commerce company had already decided that all new customer-facing applications would be developed outside their existing IT organization. According to them, IT was slow, unreliable, and prone to chaos, could not keep a delivery commitment, and got everything wrong. All they wanted in a new CIO was someone who would get their IT operations and processes in good enough shape to support the new applications that were being developed by someone else. From my perspective, this seemed like a nice, simple job: no new projects to manage (someone from outside the IT organization was managing the outsourced product development projects), no large development staff to manage, no methodology to define and track. I would come in, assess IT's process failings, implement operational and execution best practices, and let someone else handle the wave of new applications.

Exactly one week before my start date, Mitch, the company president, called me.

"Can you come in and meet with me?" he asked.

"Sure, when?"

"Right now. In fact, the sooner you can get here, the better."

My soon-to-be-vacated office was a ten-minute drive away. "I am on my way."

Mitch welcomed me into his office, sat me at his table, took a chair next to me, and placed a spreadsheet in front of me.

"As you know, we decided to outsource our new product development to a local software development company. They have been working on our projects for several months and are still months away from delivering anything. Today, I asked for a report on what we have spent so far." He pointed to the spreadsheet. "As you can see, we are spending lots of money and not getting anything for it."

I looked at the numbers on the spreadsheet—these new projects were running at a burn rate of hundreds of thousands of dollars a month. I leaned back, faced the company president, and asked, "Do they have any projections on when something will be done?"

"No. The project manager is telling me that they keep running into problems."

I thought for a moment. "Do you trust the project manager?"

"I used to but now I am not so sure. What I need right now is for you to dive into this and figure out what is going on. I know you are not yet our employee but we can't keep spending money this way. If you have time in the next week, I would appreciate it if you can talk to whomever you can—the project manager, the company doing the work, anyone—just to get a sense of where we are."

I told Mitch that I would immediately start my analysis and give him, on my official start date, a report of my suggested next steps. As the meeting was ending, I could not help but remind him. "I am happy to do this for you but this does change the terms of my employment?"

Mitch looked a little shocked. "How is that?"

"When you hired me you told me that I would have nothing to do with these development projects. I accepted that and figured that I would do one of two things. If the projects were successful, I would applaud. If the projects were challenged, I would offer my critiques. It seems I might end up doing more—and possibly quite a bit more—than that."

Because I said this last bit with a smile on my face, Mitch, too, smiled and said, "Just let me know what we need to do. These projects are critical to our success and we need them to go well."

As I drove back to my office, I thought about how my simple new job was about to change. Not only had I inherited an IT team with low credibility and low morale, I was on the verge of owning an entire portfolio of challenged projects. Where should I start? How was I going to pull this off?

For my next step, I met with Kevin, the manager of the troubled projects. Because I am a pretty matter-of-fact person, I asked, "Mitch thinks these projects are in serious trouble. Are they?"

Kevin replied, "Mitch does not have a lot of experience in large software projects. He doesn't understand that there is a lot of preparation work we have to do before we can actually produce anything. We spent a lot of time and money writing up the requirements and then validating them."

In the back of mind I started thinking, "Okay, they have decided to use traditional software development methods. We are going to create requirements documents, get them approved, and then start building software—which is fine as long as the requirements never change."

I then asked, "Have the requirements changed very much since you started?"

Kevin answered, "Yes. We did our initial requirements documents and then used them in a series of internal focus groups. The focus groups changed quite a few things and so we updated the requirements. We then used the new requirements with a small group of customers. They gave us lots of really insightful feedback and so we updated our requirements again. That is where we are now."

"So while all of this requirements gathering, creating the requirements documents, getting feedback, changing the requirements documents, getting more feedback, and then changing the requirements work was going on, what were the contract software developers doing? It seems from the monthly costs that they were doing something."

"The developers were working on the product. We have really aggressive timelines on this project and so don't have time to not be working."

Now I was starting to get really depressed. We had wasted months of time and lots of money on "churn"—people working hard but not getting anything meaningful done.

My next stop was at the offices of the contract software development company that was doing the bulk of the work on the new products—business analysis, documentation, architecture, software development, and quality assurance. I met with the company president, his chief architect, their project manager, lead business analyst, and the vice president of sales.

I started by explaining the reason for my visit. I was trying to get a handle on the project's scope and deliverables. The assembled masses gave me an overview of their company and what work had been done. I started to ask some of my deeply probing questions:

"What software development methodology do you use?"

Having done some research into my background, they proudly answered, "Agile." This is an iterative methodology.

Hmm. Agile. Yet they are developing massive amounts of throw-away code and have delivered nothing. How could or should I ask my questions without offending the group? After all, I might need their resources to get some real work done.

"Agile? That is great. That will really help me understand the current status of the projects. Can you show me the current iteration plan for one of the projects?"

They all looked at each other. Finally the chief architect answered, "We are in the process up updating our iteration plans and so don't really have anything to show you."

I replied, "That makes sense. If you are updating your iteration plans, you must be doing so from your project backlogs. Can I see one of your project backlogs? That would really help me understand the scope of the projects."

Again, silence. The business analyst eventually answered, "I can get you the requirements documents."

"Thank you. That would be fantastic."

The business analyst left the room and came back a few minutes later. "Sorry," she said, "I had to wait for the printer to warm up."

She handed me a short stack of paper. I took the first document, opened it, and started to read. It was very high level. All it described was the purpose of the application and intended audience. No pictures. No wireframes. No story maps. Just words about some nebulous product concepts and goals.

I tried not to look too stunned. "Is this what you are using to guide the architecture and development?"

She answered, "Well, not really. But it is our starting point."

"Can I see something a little more developed than the starting point?"

She gave a somewhat disgusted sigh, "We are using Agile. We use these documents to get things started and then the development teams start coding."

I thanked them for their time and drove back to my office. Now I was not only depressed but overwhelmed. A couple of days before I even started my new job, my list of issues now included:

- The IT team has no credibility.
- The IT team has no morale.
- The company has a large portfolio of software projects that are critical to its success and has outsourced those projects to a company that thinks Agile is a license to produce nothing.
- The new projects are heading toward complete failure.

- I now own this mess.
- I wonder if it is too late to get my old job back.

I was supposed to start my new job on Monday. I asked the company president, Mitch, if I could meet with him on Friday to give him my report. Given his anxiety about these projects, he carved out some time in his schedule.

I gave him a quick rundown on the issues. Most of the work that had been done was wasted. The best thing to do was to start over. He could keep his current project manager and the outsourced development company but he needed someone to rigorously guide their work—otherwise the chaos and waste would continue.

Mitch reflected for a minute and said, "That is what I thought was happening. I am glad you are here. I need you to provide that guidance."

"But," I said, "My role with these projects was to applaud their success or critique their failure. I have plenty to do just to get the IT team in shape. Don't burden me with this."

This time Mitch was the one who smiled, "If not you, who? If not now, when? We have to get these projects right and we have to have a functional IT team. I will see you on Monday. Please let me know if you need anything from me. I am glad you are here."

Thus started what became one of the most challenging and gratifying roles in my career. As I now describe the actions we took, reflect on the Trust-Ownership Model, as it was our operating system for everything we did. For each issue we encountered, for every opportunity we identified, we handled it by asking ourselves how it would affect or how it would improve trust and ownership.

With a better understanding of the project portfolio nightmare I faced, I now needed to better understand the issues with the IT team. I inherited the typical IT organizational structure. There were directors of software engineering, quality assurance, service desk, release management, program management, and operations (system and network administration). I also inherited 17 open positions in the department that we could not fill (but more on that later). I spent my first several days doing nothing but talking with people. I did not say much. Instead, I asked open-ended questions like: What do you think the issues are? What do you enjoy about working here? And my personal favorite, if you could change one thing about life in IT, what would it be?

As a result of these conversations, I wrote down my thoughts as to the reasons for the low performance and morale:

- The former CIO had been not just a micromanager but a tyrannical micromanager. He did not just insist that things be done his way. If anyone made a mistake, he threatened them with losing their jobs.
- As a result of the tyrannical micromanagement, everyone was defensive and looked for ways to shift blame to someone else.
- Some of the processes required by the tyrannical micromanager simply did not work. Most people knew these processes did not work but remained obedient lest they get fired.
- No one in the department had any idea as to the goals and priorities of the company. Not one of the IT directors could tell me what mattered to the company. They came to work, did their jobs, and went home. There was no ownership and no passion.

On top of all that, I also owned a portfolio of failed projects. Where in the world should we start?

It was clear from my spending one-on-one time with people that trust and ownership were nonexistent. Individual initiative had been beaten out of everyone—at least those still in the department. But how could we improve trust and ownership while also fixing some of the process issues that were killing our credibility?

For example, we did two production releases of our staff- and customer-facing applications each week. Our process for testing and validating the software prior to release was so bad that at least one of these releases always failed. It was nice that we were releasing new features and enhancements twice a week but what would you think of an IT department that, when they gave you a new version of your mission-critical application, brought your system down? How much credibility would they have if this happened each and every week? How much would you trust them to work on your new projects? It was no wonder that the company had decided to outsource its new projects to someone else.

In prioritizing what had to change, I started with our production validation and release process.

On the Tuesday of my first week, there was a production release that failed. I let the team scramble around to fix the problems with the release but scheduled a meeting for Wednesday.

I started by doing something very important. I did not look for anyone to blame. I did not yell at anyone. I did not express any disappointment. Rather, I asked two questions:

- Are you satisfied with our current production validation and release process?
- If not, what would you change to make it better?

Now, over the years, I have learned to master production validation and release. I am really good at the best practices way to flawlessly get any change to any system into production. I could have told them exactly how to change the process so they would never again have a problem with production release. But I had two goals: to improve our process performance *and* build a high-performing IT team. I could achieve the first goal if I told them what to do but not the second. And if I told them how to implement a best-practice production release process, it would be my process and they would never feel any ownership for it or its results.

At first, it was hard to get them to answer either of these two questions. The tyrannical micromanager had never asked their opinion on anything. But I persisted and refused to give them the answers.

The director of quality assurance, Tom, who had been with the company for only three months, finally ventured an answer:

"I think we can do it better."

I interjected, "If so, what could we do differently?"

Tom continued, "One of the problems is that our test and staging environments don't match our production environment. When we do testing, we don't test against the conditions of the production environment."

The director of operations, who, in theory, owned the test, staging, and production environments, thought he was being blamed and shot back with, "The developers make changes to the test and staging environments and don't tell me or my team what they did. Unless you give me complete control of those environments, I cannot be responsible for what happens."

The legacy blame culture was emerging, so I jumped in, "None of you know me very well but let me tell you something that really matters to me. I honestly believe that it is impossible to learn and improve if we blame others. As soon as we feel blamed, we get defensive. As soon as we are defensive, we close ourselves to new ideas. I want you to do me a favor. If you ever see or hear me blaming anyone, call me on it. I work hard to not blame anyone but it sometimes slips through. As a recovering blame-oholic, you are my support team.

"Now, let's get back to talking about how we can improve our production release process. It seems one of our opportunities is to get better at synchronizing our test, staging, and production environments. I suspect that is something we will have to get better at over time. Are there things we can do now?"

The director of release management, Sue, offered, "If the environments are not synchronized, we have to be more rigorous in our testing."

"Do we require that all of the changes be tested before they are promoted into production?" I asked.

"We suggest it but don't require it. When we talked about it before, we decided it would slow things down too much."

The quality assurance manager now said, "Is it better to do things fast or to do things right? It seems our biggest problem is releases that break. Think of how much time we spent yesterday afternoon trying to fix the broken release. I would rather do it right and not go through the weekly panic we do now."

I looked around the room and sensed general agreement. "Okay. Are we saying that one of rules is that we don't push untested changes to production?" Everyone agreed and so I asked, "Is there anything we should require? What if the change was tested but still, for some reason, breaks?"

The group was starting to get the hang of thinking. Someone answered, "When something does break in production, it is a huge pain to figure out how to either fix or reverse the change. What if there had to be a way to roll back the change?"

"Is it reasonable to require a roll-back plan as part of the release planning? Or will people think we are just trying to discourage changes?" I asked.

The director of software engineering said, "Anyone can define how to reverse a change—this is not a big deal."

And there we had it. The group came up with the plan for how to improve one of our most nagging process and performance issues. And they owned it because it was their plan. I offered my full support and asked them what I could do to help the new process succeed. All they wanted me to do was to turn down anyone who went around the process and came to me directly to beg for an exception. For me, that was an easy commitment to make.

Within one week, we no longer had any failed production releases. Our internal and external customers were shocked and delighted.

As an aside, about eight months later, one of our supposedly fully redundant network service providers suffered an outage that affected us. That was the first outage we had experienced since we changed our production release process. Our credibility had grown so much in those eight months that everyone assumed the outage was due to something beyond our control—we were the IT team whose production systems never failed. The organization was gaining confidence in us.

A few months before I started my new job, the company had conducted an employee satisfaction survey. The IT department had scored the lowest of any company department on this survey and so I knew there were plenty of internal issues we had to address. In addition, the survey asked everyone in the company their satisfaction with the various support departments—Human Resources, Accounting, Maintenance, and IT. Once again, IT had the lowest customer satisfaction score. Not only did the IT staff hate life, everyone in the company hated IT.

I knew I had to grow the ownership in the IT team to improve both our internal culture and our project results and customer service. Because I wanted to introduce myself to the entire team, I scheduled a meeting—lunch included—with the entire department. I gave everyone a short description of my background and then explained the things that mattered most to me:

- Building a high-trust, high-ownership culture.
- Delivering what mattered most to the company and doing meaningful work.

I told them that I wanted to do a potentially crazy exercise. If it was a complete failure, we would eat lunch and forget it ever happened. If it worked, we would develop an action plan for building our high-trust, high-ownership culture and then eat lunch.

We were in a large conference room filled with round tables. Naturally, people were sitting together, by department, at the tables. The operations team was in the far back of the room. The quality assurance team was at the front. The software developers were in the middle. I distributed pens and stacks of sticky notes to each table and described what would happen next.

"I want you to use your sticky notes to answer a question. Write one answer on one sticky note. Every idea you have deserves its own sticky note. Now, the question I want you to answer is:

'If you could change one thing about life in our IT department, what would it be?'

Remember, one answer per sticky. Go!"

I let them work for a few minutes. Some people wrote down one or two answers. Others wrote down dozens. When everyone had at least one answer, I told them what came next.

"I want you, one person at a time, to come to the front of the room, read what is on your sticky notes and stick them to the wall. You don't need to explain your answers; just read them out."

With some prompting, the first few people walked up, read their answers, stuck their notes on the wall, and sat back down. Soon, there was a line of people waiting to read their answers. I begged people to move quickly, as this is usually the most time-consuming part of this collaboration exercise. The answers included things like:

- Poor facilities.
- Too many interruptions.
- No priorities.
- I want to work from home.
- Get paid more.
- Kill the outsourced projects.

The next step in their collaboration process was, in silence, to group all of these answers into common concerns and opportunities. I asked anyone with a passion to come to the wall—the wall that was now covered in sticky notes—and, without saying a word, group the answers. I reminded everyone that if they trusted the people doing the grouping, they could stay where they were, but if they wanted a voice in the grouping, they should come forward. Eight people stepped up quickly and completed the grouping. I only had to remind them a few times about the "group in silence" rule.

When they finished, we had four logical categories. These were

- Working Conditions (office space, gym facilities, work from home, et cetera).
- Prioritization (what matters most, stop the interruptions, project inception, project trade-offs, et cetera).

- Internal Processes (agile or waterfall, project management, automated testing, et cetera).
- Career Development (training, pay, promotions, cross-training, et cetera).

With the reminder that we would soon serve lunch, I put the resulting categories on each wall of the room. The Working Conditions sticky notes were on the wall behind me. The Prioritization category was on the wall to my right. And so on.

I described what would happen next. "If you have a passion for identifying ways to improve our working conditions, I want you to come to the wall behind me. If you have a passion for changing how we do prioritization, go to the wall to my right. If your passion is internal processes, back there. If it's career development, over there. When you get to your category, I want you to once again use sticky notes to write down every idea you have for improving that category. And remember, one idea per sticky note. One last thing, because you are sitting by department, I would love for you to work with someone outside your department on this next part of the exercise."

Chaos ensued as everyone moved to the category of their choice, but they were soon hard at work on generating ideas for improving their category. When everyone was done, I asked them to group their improvement ideas in silence. When that was done, I added a wrinkle.

"Now I want you to vote on which of your subgroups are the highest priorities in your category. To determine the number of votes you have, take the number of subgroups in your category, divide it by three, and round up to the nearest whole number. If you have seven subgroups, seven divided by three and rounded up to the nearest whole number is three. Thus, each person gets three votes. You can use all of those votes on one or spread them around. What you cannot do is sell your votes!"

Within a few minutes, each team had its category prioritized. I asked each team to nominate a spokesperson to review the top three improvement ideas in their category. I then led them through the final step.

"We have four categories and a total of twelve improvement ideas. I now want you to vote on which of these improvement ideas are the most important to you. Because there are twelve improvement ideas, how many votes do each of you get?"

Being the smart IT professionals that they were, they were quick with the answer, "Four." I congratulated them for the answer and they voted.

When the dust settled, we had a short list of high-priority improvement ideas:

- Get good at agile software development.
- Force the company to prioritize our work.
- Give us more money.
- Give us flexible work time.
- Pay for training and certifications.

Now, I did not want to be the person who owned these improvement initiatives, so as lunch was being delivered to the back of the conference room, I announced, "Our last step is for anyone who has a passion for implementing these ideas to raise your hands. Who wants to implement getting good at agile software development?"

A few of the software engineers, quality assurance engineers, and project managers raised their hands.

"Okay, who is your team leader?"

They looked at each other and finally one person, Tim, timidly raised his hand.

"Tim, you get this team together and develop an action plan for how we will get good at agile software development. If you need help with the elements of an action plan let me know. If anyone else wants to participate on this team, please get with Tim."

I then did the same with the others ideas and asked everyone to get their lunch.

After the meeting, I met with the team leaders to answer any questions they had about their role. I told them that we would meet as a combined group once a month to conduct various departmental business (and eat lunch together). During this meeting, I asked each team leader to give a report on the status of their projects to improve life in IT.

When I met with the leader of the "Give us more money" team, he asked how likely it was that we could ever convince the company to pay the people in IT more money. In other words, was his team living in a fantasy? I asked questions to probe why money was such a big issue. Were we paying that much less than market rates? Or was money a placeholder for other, poor working conditions? If so, what were they and what could we do about them? I tried not to give him any answers. Instead, I asked him to look beyond the symptoms to see if there was a different root cause.

Some of the people in the IT group thought that this entire exercise was a waste of time—nothing had ever changed and nothing would ever change. I accepted this attitude. Behavior and culture change is long, hard work. All I could do was what I could do. I should not expect that everyone would join me on this journey—I just needed enough to get a critical mass.

But I had laid down my markers. We were all accountable for changing the culture of IT. Everyone was an owner in this transition. And I was not the person with all the answers. I was turning over a lot of trust to the teams. One team was going to define how the company would prioritize IT projects. Another would define and implement a flexible-time policy—in a company that thought that the IT group was composed of a group of slackers and miscreants who wanted to do as little as possible.

With the plan for the collaborative changing of the culture in progress, I turned a portion of my attention to sorting through what to do with that portfolio of outsourced and troubled projects.

Clearly we had to improve our delivery of these projects. But did we first need to determine whether or not those projects would actually generate business value? Seven different teams were working on supposedly high-impact projects. But would each of these projects deliver value? If so, were there ways to increase the value?

To get answers to these questions, I arranged a series of meetings with my management team peers and the company president. I started each meeting by drawing a picture of and describing the Purpose-Based Alignment Model and asking, "For us, what belongs in the Differentiating quadrant? How do we create competitive advantage? What do we have to do better than anyone else?"

Their answers were all different but centered around one basic idea: We provide the highest levels of personalized service in the industry.

This was something I could work with, and I started to use, as a project portfolio decision filter, this question:

Will [this] help us be the best in the world at personalized service?

I met with Kevin, the person managing the outsource projects, and talked him through purpose alignment. "Kevin, before we go any further on these projects, I want to rationalize the portfolio with this decision filter. Just to humor me, let's talk about one of your most challenging projects. Which is the project that troubles you the most?"

He answered, "Clearly our integration service. We need something to pass transactional information among the various application modules and components. We spent a lot of time looking at the options but were not really happy with the available technologies and so are developing a new messaging platform."

"Are you using standard messaging technologies or will they not work?"

"According to our analysis, they won't work—thus, the project. I have the best developers on the team working on this because everything hinges off it working."

I tried to sort through how to ask my next question and decided to just plunge in. "Let's use our decision filter on the project. Will an advanced, unique messaging platform help us be the best in the world at personalized customer service?"

Kevin answered, "It might."

I asked back, "How?"

"We have to get it right or everything else fails."

"Kevin, you know how difficult it is to write and test software. You have been doing this for a long time. And you think that using an unproven, to-be-developed technology is the best way to get a proven, must-be-right result? Again, let me ask, will developing our own messaging technology help us be better than anyone else at personalized service? To be honest, I cannot see any connection at all. The messaging is mission critical but hardly something we do to create competitive advantage. Given that, we should apply the parity rules and find the simplest, most standard, and best-practices-based option that exists. We are certainly not the only people who need to exchange mission-critical transactional data."

Kevin pushed forward, "But we looked at other options and we don't think they will work."

"Remember the goal of parity—and this is clearly parity—is to find something that works well enough. For data exchange, such tools exist because they are an essential building block of any enterprise system. Who on the outsourced team did the search for existing tools?"

Kevin replied, "The chief architect."

"Perfect. I will talk with him."

I called the outsource provider's architect. "Jason, do you remember me? We met at your office a couple of weeks ago."

"Sure. What can I do for you?"

"Jason, I am looking at some of the project elements and have some questions about the messaging platform. I was wondering why you decided to build your own."

Jason answered, "Oh, that. One of the guys on my team had a really great idea for a new messaging architecture. We think it will offer you a superior solution."

"That sounds great. How is the development going?"

"Well, it works really well at low transaction volumes but suffers a bit when we apply more load. We think we will have the problems worked out pretty soon."

"Jason, don't worry about it. Let's stop working on it right now."

Jason was stunned, "Stop? But we've put a lot of effort into this project."

"Yes. I know. I have seen the budget and the invoices. We don't need a superior messaging platform. We need something that is proven. Even if your team works it out, we will be left with a custom messaging platform to support and enhance for the rest of our lives. That is something I don't want to take on."

Jason took a new approach, "But if we stop now, you will have wasted the thousands of developer hours we have already spent getting it to where it is."

"Jason, I understand. How many hours do you estimate it will take to get it done?"

I had just raised Jason's hopes. "My team estimates 800 to 1,000 more hours."

"Jason, I cannot afford to waste another 800 to 1,000 developer hours on a product I don't need. Let's kill it now and apply those talented, smart resources to something we really need."

I then talked to my director of software engineering and asked him to find a market-leading messaging platform we could use as our standard. He came back a day later with a purchase requisition in hand. For a cost that was much less than thousands of software developer hours and a simple download, we had our messaging platform.

I got the team to apply the purpose alignment and our decision filter to everything in the outsourced project portfolio.

One of the projects was to deliver a customer profile application. The assigned team had already spent thousands of hours creating a unique and innovative customer profile application. This project had a potential connection to how we created competitive advantage but did it require custom, unique development? While our customer profile application was important, there was no direct connection between it and being the best at personalized service. Why, then, were we creating a very innovative customer profile application? Because we did not know better. Would making a unique and interesting customer profile application generate value for us? No chance. Doing a better customer profile would not do a single thing to help us win in the marketplace. True, our customer profile application had to be good—its function was mission critical—but customers were not going to do business with us because we excelled at defining their profiles. After placing the project in the Parity category, I now had to align the project to that placement. In a kind and gentle way, I thanked the team for their work and effort and told them that I was killing the project and replacing it with a standard configuration of our customer relationship management system's profile features.

This change in approach optimized value. The highest-value way for us to deliver a profile application was to use something that already existed and worked really well.

As a result, we stopped three of the seven outsourced projects and dramatically simplified the other four. Even better, we started to take ownership of our destiny. The company started to think that we knew what we were doing and just might do a better job of new product development than they had thought. Over the next few months, we shifted our developers into the lead positions on the remaining four outsourced projects, got them back on track, and delivered them.

With the goal of increasing trust and ownership to get to Energy and Innovation, the IT team had taken ownership (and I trusted them) to improve internal processes. We had also aligned the external project portfolio. There was still one major missing piece—we did not yet have ownership for the company's results. We needed to align everything we did to the company's goals. But what were those goals? In a perfect world, everyone in the IT group would be able to map what they were doing to one of the company's goals.

I again hit the road and met with everyone on the leadership team. I explained that I wanted to make sure that IT was focused on helping each one of them achieve their goals. To do that, I needed to understand their goals—both in the short and the long term.

I synthesized their answers. I then gave the entire management team a report on my understanding of the goals so that we could all agree. We agreed to three high-level goals:

- Increase customer retention.
- Improve profit margins.
- Become an employer of choice—attract and retain the best employees.

(Now, you might wonder why I had this meeting without members of my IT staff. At this point the IT group was still the gang that could not shoot straight.)

With these goals defined, I asked my entire IT team to map their work to these goals. I met with each group to inventory their current projects. We then identified which of the three goals, if any, the projects supported. We had plenty of orphan projects and so put those on temporary hold—at least until their project sponsors could map them to one of the company goals.

At our next all-staff meeting, I introduced and explained the company goals to everyone in the IT group and showed them which projects mapped to the goals and which did not. We then discussed any projects we should be doing that would help achieve the company goals. These went onto our project backlog. In my spare time, I created a visual display that showed each current IT project and which company goal it supported. We published this graphic to the entire company so that they could see not only what we were doing but why we were doing it. Finally, we revised our project inception process to consider how the proposed project mapped to the three goals. At each of our all-staff meetings, we updated the project visual with our progress and reminded each other of the company goals.

One of the projects we added to our backlog was advanced customer analytics. Because one of goals was increased customer retention, we decided we needed to better understand customer behaviors. Which customers stayed with us? Why? Which customer left? Why? Would it be possible for us to identify at-risk customers and then do an intervention to keep them? Was this worth doing? How did this project align with our decision filter? If we were to be better than anyone else at personalized service, shouldn't part of that service be knowing when it was time to rescue a customer? Or make sure we provided services that meant no customer ever had to be rescued?

Because this project aligned with our Differentiating activities, we figured we should do something innovative. In our minds, that allowed us to be somewhat experimental. We brainstormed some of the things we could try and decided which ones to pursue. In some cases, we experimented with proven technologies. In other cases, we developed very low-cost pilots of our ideas. Some things worked but most failed. When we found something that might work, we started to communicate what we were doing (until then, the project was an IT "skunk works" project). Because we were dealing with so much uncertainty, we used iterative methods. We selected some pilot data from pilot customers and did more experiments. We gathered feedback and results and planned our next test. When we published our first working results, the company was ecstatic. They had insight into customer behavior that they never thought was possible.

On the increasing trust side of life, I used every tool we describe in this book. I never gave answers—even when I knew the answers. I trusted first. When I started the job, the company president asked me how many members of the IT group I would have to fire to improve the team's performance. Not wanting to make a commitment when I knew the least, I gave a nebulous answer. My assumption was that everyone wanted to do a great job but was being stopped by leadership or process or something. I expressed thanks when people did well. I expressed thanks when people pretty much did anything. When someone made a mistake, I asked them what they had learned from the experience. I kept my commitments. If I was not sure I could commit to something, I told them so. I wanted to be completely trustworthy.

When it was time to do our annual budget, I discovered that my directors had never done budgeting. The tyrannical micromanager had done it all himself. I met with the person who owned the budgeting process and asked him to create a separate budget for each of my directors (under the regime of the tyrannical micromanager, there were not departmental budgets—just one big IT group budget). We allocated the current expenses as best we could to the various, new budgets. We then met with the IT directors and set them loose. I told them that it was nearly impossible to make a mistake, just to put in what we needed and we could adjust from there. When their budgets came in, they had been very conservative, so we had the joy of brainstorming ideas for what to do with the money they did not need (like fund our customer analytics and intervention experiments).

We replaced detailed, personal metrics with process metrics, such as: Did we keep our commitments? Did we provide outstanding customer service? Were we a great place to work?

Was it all so easy and happy? Hardly. Culture change never is. It made a huge, immediate difference just to ask people their opinions as to what we should do. We still had some fundamental process, trust, and credibility problems to solve but now we were in it together.

As I mentioned, on the day I started, there were 17 open positions in IT. The company had such a bad reputation that it was impossible to hire anyone—even at the height of the 2009 economic meltdown. Naturally, I was concerned about hiring anyone into what still might be a culture of low trust and ownership. I met with our internal and external recruiters and explained what we were doing, how the culture was changing. I asked them to find me candidates that fit into the culture we were creating—not the culture we had. I met with each job candidate in person and described the future. This would be a culture of trust and ownership. I told them that their jobs would not only include job tasks but would also be to change the culture. We soon filled every open position.

Not everyone reacted well to the changes. One of my directors struggled mightily to take ownership and be trusted. Many times he told me, "Just tell me what to do!" Over time, he became more and more uncomfortable with the culture and found a new job. But almost everyone else embraced the changes and thrived. How do we know?

Six months later, we did a new employee survey; IT employee satisfaction and company satisfaction with IT had increased by nearly 25 percent. Project throughput (a measure of how many projects we completed per unit time) had doubled. Best of all, we had become the IT supplier of choice to the company. Before trust and ownership, everyone looked for ways to not use the IT group. Now, everyone wanted us to take on their projects. Even better, people were willing to delay their projects in order to wait for the IT teams to be available. We still had a long way to go but we were clearly on our way to Energy and Innovation.

QUICK REFERENCE GUIDE

How do you begin? Start with the assessment of where you are in the Trust-Ownership Model. Then, use the tools in Table A.1 to move to Energy and Innovation.

Because many of the tools can serve a dual purpose, we created the matrix in Table A.1, which lists the tools and where they apply to moving toward trust, ownership, business alignment, and dealing honestly with ambiguity. We also reference the chapter where details about each tool can be found.

Table A.1   Tools to Move to Energy and Innovation

Tool	Trust	Ownership	Alignment	Ambiguity	Chapter
Culture of Trust	Yes				4
Don't Give Answers—Ask Questions		Yes			5
Don't Correct Mistakes		Yes			5
Help Teams Take Ownership		Yes			5
Macro-Leadership Cube		Yes		Yes	5
Purpose-Based Alignment Model		Yes	Yes		6
Business Value Model		Yes	Yes	Yes	6
Inception Planning	Yes	Yes	Yes	Yes	6
Proactive Risk Management		Yes		Yes	7
Iterative Methods				Yes	7
Value Driven, Not Date Driven	Yes			Yes	8
Managing Up	Yes	Yes			8
Collaborating with Non-Collaborators	Yes	Yes		Yes	8
Measuring Culture Change	Yes	Yes	Yes	Yes	9

TRUST-OWNERSHIP ASSESSMENT

Team Questions on Trust and Ambiguity

As a team member, select a number between 1 and 10 that best reflects where you are.

Low (1–3)	Medium (4–7)	High (8–10)	Your Score
I have to get permission to do anything.	Managers and processes sometimes get in my way.	I am trusted to do my work.	_____
I am told what to do and how to do it.	I can sometimes find my own solution.	I am trusted to always be able to find my own solution.	_____
If I don't do things the approved way, I am at risk.	There are certain low-risk things I can do.	I can take chances without feeling at risk.	_____
I always must give the organization exact numbers.	I sometimes can tell the organization when I am uncertain.	I can honestly tell the organization when I am uncertain without risk.	_____
		Average Trust Score	_____

Average the averages of all team members. This will tell where the team thinks it is on the y-axis—Trust—on the model.

Team Questions on Ownership and Alignment

As a team member, select a number between 1 and 10 that best reflects where you are.

Low (1–3)	Medium (4–7)	High (8–10)	Your Score
We are told how to do our work.	Our team can define parts of the solution.	Our team has full ownership of the solution.	_____
I don't know what the goals are.	I understand some of the goals.	I clearly understand the organization's business goals.	_____
What's a value proposition?	I think I understand some of the value proposition.	I clearly understand and agree to the value proposition for my project.	_____
I'll only get something done if I know someone is going to ask me for it.	I feel responsible for small parts of the project.	I feel personally accountable for delivering on the organization goals.	_____
I don't see how my work connects to organizational goals.	In some cases I can connect my work to organizational goals.	I can directly link my work to organizational purpose and goals.	_____
		Average Ownership Score	_____

Average the averages of all team members. This tells you where the team is on the x-axis—Ownership.

Leader Questions on Trust and Ambiguity

As the team leader, select a number between 1 and 10 that best reflects where you are.

Low (1–3)	Medium (4–7)	High (8–10)	Your Score
I trust no one on my team.	I trust some of my team.	I trust my entire team.	_____
I require that everything must be defined before the team can do anything.	The big things, such as cost, schedule, and scope, must be defined before the team can do anything.	I honestly accept and allow genuine ambiguity and uncertainty from my team.	_____
My team cannot take risks without my approval.	I let my team take risks—but only when the risks are low.	I encourage my team to take risks in order to deliver value more effectively.	_____
		Average Trust Score	_____

Leader Questions on Ownership and Alignment

As the team leader, select a number between 1 and 10 that best reflects where you are.

Low (1–3)	Medium (4–7)	High (8–10)	Your Score
It's my neck on the line. They better do what I tell them to do.	My team can own some parts of the solution.	My team has ownership of the entire solution.	_____
My team doesn't understand or accept the organization's goals.	My team understands some of the organization's goals.	My team understands and accepts the organization's business goals.	_____
My team doesn't understand or accept the project's goals.	My team understands some of the project's goals.	My team understands and accepts the business goals of the project.	_____
My team doesn't understand the value proposition at all.	My team gets the small picture but I own the big picture.	My team understands and accepts the project's value proposition.	_____
		Average Ownership Score	_____

Mark Your Positions

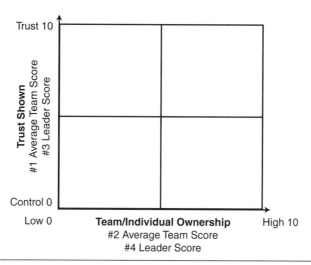

FIGURE B.1 Where are you?

Discussion Points

- Where are you on the chart?
- Do the leader and the team have the same view?
- What actions can be taken to increase trust?
- What actions can be taken to increase ownership?

COLLABORATION PROCESS

From the book, *Stand Back and Deliver: Accelerating Business Agility*, by Pollyanna Pixton, Niel Nickolaisen, Todd Little, and Kent McDonald.

What It Is

Collaboration is a powerful tool to find answers in your organization and foster the flow of ideas.

When to Use It

Use this tool to answer questions as a group that can help solve problems such as prioritizing projects and determining their purpose, increasing productivity and workflow, identifying and developing innovative products and services, and managing risk, uncertainty, and complexity.

How to Use It

Bring the right people together—those interested in the success of the issue and those impacted by the issue. Create an open environment based on trust. Use the collaboration process to stimulate the flow of ideas.

1. Agree to the goal, objective, or problem to be solved.
2. Using sticky notes and marking pens, everyone brainstorms their answers, one answer on one sticky note, as many notes as they need.
3. Have each person read their answers out loud to the group as they stick each note on the wall or whiteboard.

4. Ask the entire team to group the notes—in silence. Give them no other directions than that.
5. As a team, have them label the groups with a title they all agree to.
6. Add up the number of groups, divide by three, and round up. This is the number of votes each person has to vote for the most important or best solution.
7. Let each person vote next to the title. Make sure they understand that they can put more than one vote on a group if they feel it has great importance to them.
8. Tally the votes.
9. Break them into smaller teams and work on how you can implement the highest-voted groups, with each breakout team taking a different group and then reporting their results to the full team.
10. Work through all relevant groups.
11. Let people decide what tasks they want to do and by when. Stress that they should take on tasks they want to do. The remaining tasks that no one wants to do should be resolved by the full team.

In leading this collaboration effort, remember to use questions to keep the focus, stand back and let people work, trust first, avoid rescuing the team, practice influence not command and control, over communicate, and listen.

COLLABORATING WITH NON-COLLABORATORS WORKSHEET

Think of a Non-Collaborator You Struggle With

Leader? ☐

Team Member? ☐

Other Team? ☐

Process? ☐

What Are the Traits (Behaviors) of Your Non-Collaborator?

What Type Is Your Non-Collaborator?

Check as many as apply. There might be more than one.

❑ Doesn't know how to collaborate

❑ Afraid to collaborate

❑ "It's all about me!"

What Makes Your Non-Collaborator Tick?

■ What is his or her focus?

■ What is his or her motivation?

■ How does he or she define success?

■ What is his or her team's definition of success?

■ What is his or her reward system?

- How is he or she acknowledged?

- What are his or her fears?

- What are his or her "hot buttons"?

- Does he or she have any hidden agendas?

What Makes You Tick?

- How do you define success?

- What are you passionate about?

- What do you do best?

- What do you fear?

Where Are You Compared to Your Non-Collaborator?

For each line in the following diagram, mark where you sit and where your non-collaborator sits.

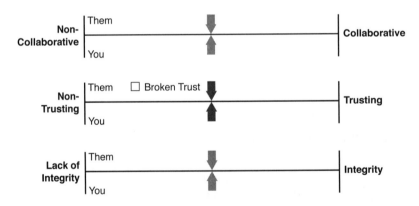

Why Do You Want to Collaborate with This Non-Collaborator?

❏   For business purposes.

❏   You need information for your team to succeed.

❏   Your non-collaborator needs to take action.

❏   Your non-collaborator needs to stand back.

❏   You want to change your non-collaborator.

❏   You want to remove your non-collaborator .

Manage Your Risks

What are your risks? Can you

❏   Let someone else take the credit for your ideas and accomplishments?

❏   Survive without your mentors?

❏   Deal with any undeserved, negative labels?

❏   Deal with public humiliation?

❏   Handle your career being derailed in this organization?

❏   Handle being fired?

❏   Find another job as good or better within three months?

What are your professional options (beyond this role)?

1.

2.

3.

List some successful risks taken in the past:

-
-
-
-

Dealing with Non-Collaborators

Where Is Your Non-Collaborator?

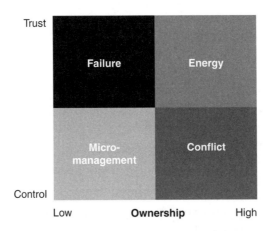

Can Your Non-Collaborator Ever Collaborate?

❑ Yes = Work to build collaborative behavior.
❑ No = Work around them and try to mitigate the damage.

What Actions Are You Going to Take?

What techniques do you want to try?

-
-
-
-
-

WHAT TO DO ABOUT METRICS

A Detailed Description

Now that we understand the characteristics of effective metrics, it is easy to understand how inappropriate metrics can act as walls to the team and good metrics can drive effective improvement. Poor metrics will stop teams from improving by forcing them to focus on activities that will not increase the effectiveness of their value delivery. Good metrics focus effort where it has real effect.

You can use metrics in a variety of areas—as long as they provide useful and actionable information and don't create walls.

Some of the major areas of metrics include

- Internal
- Organizational
- External

The actual metrics you choose to use will, of course, be based on your actual situation.

Internal Metrics

You gather these during the delivery cycle, and the delivery team acts on them in as close to real time as possible. The shorter the cycles, the better. To have the most positive effect, they need to be well aligned and have integrity.

Teams and individuals will align their priorities to the organization's behaviors. If the organization stresses schedule, then quality will certainly be compromised. If the organization values process adherence, then that will be more important than customer and business value delivered.

Please again consider the cost to gather and analyze the metric. To improve early defect analysis, some teams record all development-discovered Unit Test defects in their problem-tracking system. This has a huge impact on team productivity with little corresponding value.

Internal measures can be very helpful in allowing leaders and teams to improve effectiveness in target areas. Well-aligned measures are predictive. But if not well-designed, they can cause bad behavior. Internal measures should promote action at the team level.

- Good examples of internal measures
  - Technical debt
  - Test coverage (path or branch)
  - Orthogonal defect classification (ODC)[1]
- Bad examples of internal measures
  - Iteration velocity when used as a team-effectiveness metric rather than as a means to assess project progress.
  - Causal Analysis—this is very costly to use on a continuous basis.
  - Unit Test defect tracking—this has a tendency to create a lot of non-value work and bureaucracy.

Organizational Metrics

Organizational measures are used to assess the effectiveness of operations or strategies. These differ from internal metrics in that they are targeted for action beyond the individual team. There is a high risk of misuse if these are used below the organizational level. Incidentally, organizational metrics applied at the team level is one of the most common reasons that metrics get a bad name.

Cycle times for organizational metrics are typically longer than for internal metrics.

---

1. Ram Chillarege, "Orthogonal Defect Classification," http://www.chillarege.com/articles/odc-concept

An organization wanted to evaluate the effectiveness of their software development teams. The company was well aware that incorrect measures could cause bad behavior in the teams. At the same time, the organization wanted to understand the effectiveness of its investments in technology and process.

The organization settled on metrics of Lines of Code (LOC) per Programmer Month (PM) and Cost per LOC as the key measures. Their initial assumption was that there was a positive relationship (though possibly not linear) between code delivered and customer value. Because such measures are known to be dangerous and often cause bad behavior (teams feel that they are being compared to others) the company took great care in collecting and using the data. The company collected the data directly from the development libraries and averaged it, by target platform, across the whole business. This eliminated any chance of comparing teams or projects.

The raw data collected was

- **Unique lines of code in the libraries.** They used this to assess the code creation velocity of the development teams. It was clearly different by platform and by product and gave a good indication of the effectiveness of investments in tooling, training, and process enhancements. Note that it was not used to compare teams or individuals because their product profiles were quite different.
- **Lines of code being shipped in products with credit given for multiple use.** This was used to assess the effect of reuse on the delivery of business value. The results clearly showed that this was by far the most effective way of increasing value delivered to the customer.
- **Lines of code in the support libraries.** This explained support effort trends and informed the migration strategies for existing customers. This was also the measure with the fastest growth, as the company supported customers at different software levels.
- **Overall development and support staffing and costs.** This gave an indication of overall productivity and the effect of various organizational initiatives.

The company used this data to show multiple-year trends across many projects to validate and guide investments in the development process and infrastructure. As expected, the data showed significant variation in LOC productivity depending on the hardware platform and the quality requirements of the target market. There were also some interesting findings such as

- Unique LOC productivity per programmer was basically flat but assessed business value trended up sharply. The company's investment in improved infrastructure and processes enabled the move to higher-level platforms and languages and more complex systems.
- Shipped or sold LOC increased at over 18 percent per year over a decade as the company emphasized the reuse of common components across multiple products and solutions.
- Cost per LOC supported was falling fast from increased quality and investments that made it easier to produce high-quality software.

Thus, even sometimes controversial metrics can be effective if used carefully and in a way that does not compromise integrity.

- Good examples of organizational metrics
  - Aggregate Manager NPS—assessing the degree to which the managers are seen to support their development teams.
  - Average Cycle Time.
  - Profitability.
- Bad examples of organizational metrics
  - LOC per PM at a team level.

External Metrics

We use external metrics to understand the market view of a product or an organizational capability.

A common and powerful measure is the Net Promoter Score (NPS)[2] of the solutions or products being sold.

An organizational example is the Trust Index Employee Survey done by Great Place to Work.[3]

---

2. http://www.netpromotersystem.com/about/index.aspx
3. http://www.greatplacetowork.com

Each year the Great Place to Work Institute polls many companies to assess the degree of trust felt by employees. They analyze and collate this data to include in their annual report.

The survey has high levels of integrity and the institute has demonstrated very strong alignment between an organization's Trust Index and its business performance.

The survey's action cycle time is quite short and organizations take the survey once a year.

- Good examples of external metrics
  - Net Promoter Score for individual products.
- Bad examples of external metrics
  - Customer satisfaction surveys completed in the presence of the salesperson.
  - Net Promoter Score across products, which is not actionable.

Examples of Possible Metrics

We always resist the temptation to tell anyone what metrics they should use. At the same time, people beg us to give them meaningful metrics they should consider. That said, here is a list of metrics—many focused on software development (that most challenging of processes)—you can use as a starting point—but just as a starting point. To be meaningful, metrics must be yours and must change as you, your teams, and your organization progress and improve—and as the marketplace changes. To keep the example list short, we have not included detailed descriptions, as most are well known and more detail is just a search away.

- To assess organizational support of delivery
  - Organization NPS
  - Manager NPS
  - Percentage Flow Time (time without interruptions)
  - Anxiety Boredom Continuum
  - Meeting Net Promoter Score (NPS for regular meetings)
- To predict project progress
  - Earned Value
  - Story Point Burndown or Burnup
  - Function Point delivery

- To improve delivered quality and reduce technical debt
  - Open Defects at iteration end, particularly Severity 1 and 2
  - Severity 3 and 4 defects that cross two iteration boundaries
  - Unit or Regression Test Code Coverage
  - Successful test cases run
  - Orthogonal Defect Classification
- To reduce development wasted effort
  - Build Breaks
  - Integration Lag (the average time a changed module waits before build)
- To assess process effectiveness and improvement
  - Timely Iteration Completion
  - Closure of Actions from Reflections
  - Deferred User Stories
  - Cycle Time
  - Value Stream Map
- To assess organizational productivity
  - Delivered code trends—unique/shipped or sold/supported
  - Sales Velocity
- To assess practice adoption
  - Survey teams on whether they use the practice in <25%/25% to 75%/>75% of the places where it might be used.
  - Green/Amber/Red/Black assessment of progress
    - Green—data collected, meeting goal
    - Amber—data collected, not meeting goal
    - Red—data collected, not analyzed
    - Black—no data available
- To assess practice credibility
  - Practice NPS
- To evaluate customer attitudes to the product
  - Product NPS
- Business Effectiveness
  - Overall Cycle time
  - Time to Break Even
  - Time to first dollar returned
  - E/R
  - Profit & Loss
  - ROI

- NPV
- Cash Flow
- Revenue Growth
- Stakeholder NPS
- Cultural/Organizational Metrics
  - Learning from failure
  - Risk taking
  - Innovating
  - Availability of cross-functional teams
  - Participation of full team in program success
  - Trust
- Metrics for management
  - E/R
  - Head count to E/R percentage
  - Head count to products delivered
- What *not* to measure:
  - Velocity as a measure of team effectiveness
  - Technical debt as a measure of the team
  - Heroic behavior
  - Process against plan
  - Story points as hours worked

ABOUT THE AUTHORS

Pollyanna Pixton, an international collaborative leadership expert, developed the models for collaboration and collaborative leadership through her thirty-eight years of working in and consulting with corporations and organizations. She helps companies create workplaces where talent and innovation are unleashed—making them more productive, efficient, and profitable. Pollyanna is a founding partner of Accelinnova. She speaks and writes on topics such as creating cultures of trust, ownership, leading collaboration, and business agility.

Paul Gibson, who trained as an electronics engineer, has recently retired from IBM after thirty-eight years of working on IBM products and processes in many differing roles up to senior levels both in the U.K. and in the U.S. For his final ten years, in addition to his line responsibilities, Paul was on the steering group of a cross-IBM organization set up by the board to improve development effectiveness and quality delivered by all 35,000 IBM software engineers. For the last four of those years, Paul was a member of a small team leading the adoption of Agile, Lean, and Collaborative approaches across the company, and he has run training sessions in virtually every major IBM Lab worldwide, as well as worked with corporate and group process owners to help them adopt complementary approaches to improve effectiveness. Since his retirement, Paul has been providing independent consultancy to a number of client companies in the U.S., Europe, and India on development effectiveness, agility, quality, and collaborative leadership.

Niel Nickolaisen is the chief technology officer at O.C. Tanner—the leading provider of innovative cloud-based software, awards, education, and recognition solutions for more than 8,000 companies worldwide. Designed to engage talent, drive corporate goals, and increase performance, these solutions combine the power of global SaaS programs with meaningful off-line recognition experiences. Niel holds an M.S. in engineering from MIT, and a B.S. in physics and an M.B.A. from Utah State University. Niel has spent his career finding rapid, pragmatic ways to improve processes, teams, and results. He is passionate about transforming IT and leadership, and speaks about, writes about, and trains others how to do this.

Index

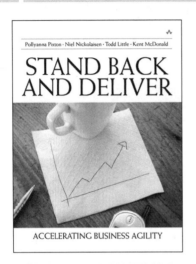

informIT.com THE TRUSTED TECHNOLOGY LEARNING SOURCE

PEARSON

InformIT is a brand of Pearson and the online presence for the world's leading technology publishers. It's your source for reliable and qualified content and knowledge, providing access to the top brands, authors, and contributors from the tech community.

✦Addison-Wesley   **Cisco Press**   EXAM/**CRAM**   **IBM** Press.   que'   ‖ PRENTICE HALL   **SAMS** | Safari'

LearnIT at InformIT

Looking for a book, eBook, or training video on a new technology? Seeking timely and relevant information and tutorials? Looking for expert opinions, advice, and tips? **InformIT has the solution.**

- Learn about new releases and special promotions by subscribing to a wide variety of newsletters.
  Visit **informit.com/newsletters**.

- Access FREE podcasts from experts at **informit.com/podcasts**.

- Read the latest author articles and sample chapters at **informit.com/articles**.

- Access thousands of books and videos in the Safari Books Online digital library at **safari.informit.com**.

- Get tips from expert blogs at **informit.com/blogs**.

Visit **informit.com/learn** to discover all the ways you can access the hottest technology content.

Are You Part of the IT Crowd?

Connect with Pearson authors and editors via RSS feeds, Facebook, Twitter, YouTube, and more! Visit **informit.com/socialconnect**.

 **informIT.com** THE TRUSTED TECHNOLOGY LEARNING SOURCE   **PEARSON**

✦Addison-Wesley   **Cisco Press**   EXAM/**CRAM**   **IBM** Press.   que'   ‖ PRENTICE HALL   **SAMS** | Safari'

    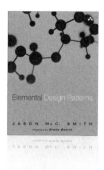

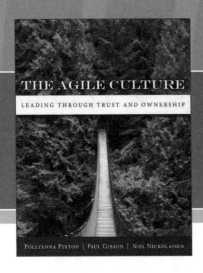

FREE
Online Edition

Your purchase of **The Agile Culture** includes access to a free online edition for 45 days through the Safari Books Online subscription service. Nearly every Addison-Wesley Professional book is available online through **Safari Books Online**, along with thousands of books and videos from publishers such as Cisco Press, Exam Cram, IBM Press, O'Reilly Media, Prentice Hall, Que, Sams, and VMware Press.

Safari Books Online is a digital library providing searchable, on-demand access to thousands of technology, digital media, and professional development books and videos from leading publishers. With one monthly or yearly subscription price, you get unlimited access to learning tools and information on topics including mobile app and software development, tips and tricks on using your favorite gadgets, networking, project management, graphic design, and much more.

Activate your FREE Online Edition at
informit.com/safarifree

STEP 1: Enter the coupon code: BWPRSZG.

STEP 2: New Safari users, complete the brief registration form.
Safari subscribers, just log in.

If you have difficulty registering on Safari or accessing the online edition,
please e-mail customer-service@safaribooksonline.com